"Imagine finding a therapist who understands anxiety and [...] kids. Imagine that therapist packaging acceptance and com[...] concepts and skills into bite-size portions and feeding them to your child with clarity, humor, and engaging art. Imagine your child taking a bite, and then another. Willingly learning skills. Going back for more. That's what Anna Scetinina has accomplished here, creating a unique ACT workbook sure to help young worriers."

—**DAWN HUEBNER, PhD,** psychologist, parent coach, and author of books, including *What to Do When You Worry Too Much* and *Outsmarting Worry*

"We know that ACT can help children and children can learn ACT, but that alone does not show you how. This book does. Funny and interesting, it playfully teaches all the key ACT skills needed to address worry. Highly recommended."

—**STEVEN C. HAYES, PhD,** Foundation Professor of Psychology Emeritus, University of Nevada, Reno; and codeveloper of ACT

"Anna Scetinina did the impossible! She took what are often complex therapy skills to address big emotions and broke them down into simple and manageable activities. Her workbook is not only clinically sound, but also engaging and fun. A must-read for anxious kids and their families!"

—**NATASHA DANIELS, LCSW,** anxiety and obsessive-compulsive disorder (OCD) child therapist, and author of *Crushing OCD Workbook for Kids*

"I wish I read this book when I was a child! This delightful workbook provides clear and effective strategies for kids to deal with difficult internal experiences, accept things they can't control, and build a flexible mindset. Not only is this book beautifully illustrated and packed with creative, fun, and engaging activities, but it also presents an amazing opportunity for parents to implement these strategies together with their kids."

—**ANNA PRUDOVSKI, MA, CPsych,** clinical psychologist, supervisor, and founder of the Turning Point Psychological Services, anxiety and OCD clinic in Ontario, Canada

"If every child embraces the empowering mindset and essential skills shared in this transformative book, our world will undoubtedly become a much better place for everyone."

—**VICTORIA PROODAY, OT Reg. (Ont.)**, occupational therapist and clinical director of Victorious Kids, a center for empowering kids and parents with skills for success

"Anna brilliantly weaves her professional experience as a psychotherapist together with her artistic talent into this playful road map to a flexible mindset for young worriers. Delightfully approachable characters and engaging activities build a fun and empowering toolkit for youth distracted from the beauty of life by their anxieties and fears. Highly recommended!"

—**SHELLEY RICHARDSON, MEd**, A.M.I. Montessori educator, owner of Richardson Montessori & Eddy Press publishing, and author of *SOPHIE and The Magic of Dance* and *RIVER: We Are Ever the Masterpiece*

A WORKBOOK for KIDS WHO WORRY

50 WAYS TO STAND UP TO WORRY

Fun Activities to Help Children Face Their Fears
and Build a Flexible Mindset
Using Acceptance and Commitment Therapy

Anna Scetinina, MACP, RP

Instant Help Books
An Imprint of New Harbinger Publications, Inc.

Publisher's Note

This publication is designed to provide accurate and authoritative information in regard to the subject matter covered. It is sold with the understanding that the publisher is not engaged in rendering psychological, financial, legal, or other professional services. If expert assistance or counseling is needed, the services of a competent professional should be sought.

NEW HARBINGER PUBLICATIONS is a registered trademark of New Harbinger Publications, Inc.

New Harbinger Publications is an employee-owned company.

Copyright © 2025 by Anna Scetinina
New Harbinger Publications, Inc.
5720 Shattuck Avenue
Oakland, CA 94609
www.newharbinger.com

All Rights Reserved

Illustrations, cover design, and interior design by Anna Scetinina

Acquired by Wendy Millstine

Edited by Elizabeth Dougherty

Printed in the United States of America

27　26　25

10　9　8　7　6　5　4　3　2　1　　　　　　　　　　　　　　First Printing

Contents

Foreword — VII
A Letter to Parents — VIII
A Note for Professionals — X
A Letter to Kids — XII

Section 1
Understanding Your Worry

Activity 1: Are You a Worrier? — 2
Activity 2: Where Do You Feel Worry in Your Body? — 4
Activity 3: Your Brain's Main Job — 6
Activity 4: Old Mind and New Mind — 8
Activity 5: Do You Have a Flexible Mindset? — 10
Activity 6: What Do You Do When You Worry? — 12
Section 1 Quiz — 15

Section 2
How to Grow a Flexible Mindset

Activity 7: Flex Park Attractions and a Flexible Mindset — 20
Activity 8: Word Search — 23
Activity 9: Toward and Away Roads — 24
Activity 10: Choosing the Toward Road — 26
Activity 11: Travel into the Future — 28
Activity 12: End Goals Versus Action Goals — 31
Activity 13: Your Feelings Thermometer — 33
Activity 14: My Worry Is Like . . . — 35
Activity 15: Notice How Your Feelings Change — 36
Section 2 Quiz — 39

Section 3
Befriend Your Worry

Activity 16: "Don't Worry"	42
Activity 17: You Can Stop Growing Worries	45
Activity 18: Meet Your Fear	48
Activity 19: Make Room for Your Worry	50
Activity 20: Blooming Flower	52
Activity 21: Your Feelings and You	54
Activity 22: Feelings Finger Puppets	57
Activity 23: Make Friends with Your Worry	58
Section 3 Quiz	63

Section 4
Unhook from Worry Thoughts

Activity 24: Facts, Ideas, and Hooks	66
Activity 25: Your Mind's Tricks	69
Activity 26: Watch Your Mind	71
Activity 27: Leaves on a Stream	72
Activity 28: The Unhooking Toolkit	75
10 Ways to Take Power Away from Your Worry Thoughts	75
Activity 29: Become an Observer	78
Activity 30: Quick Mind Mode	82
Activity 31: You Are More	84
Section 4 Quiz	87

Section 5
Mindfulness

Activity 32: What Is Mindfulness?	90
Activity 33: Being Mindful	92
Activity 34: Take a Breath	94
Activity 35: Anchor Yourself	97

Activity 36: Look, Listen, and Breathe — 101
Activity 37: The Mindfulness Toolkit — 103
10 Ways to Practice Being Mindful — 103
Activity 38: Make a Healthy Habits Checklist — 106
Section 5 Quiz — 109

Section 6
Your Heart's Secrets

Activity 39: Your Strengths — 112
Activity 40: Things That Matter — 116
Activity 41: Your Superhero Badge — 118
Activity 42: What Makes You Happy? — 120
Activity 43: Fun with What Matters — 122
Activity 44: Brave You — 124
Section 6 Quiz — 129

Section 7
You Can Do It

Activity 45: Set a SMART Goal — 132
Activity 46: Jump Over Obstacles — 134
Activity 47: Your Plan for Dealing with Worry — 137
Activity 48: Be Kind to Yourself — 140
Activity 49: Being Kind Tic-Tac-Toe — 143
Activity 50: How Flexible Are You Now? — 145
Section 7 Quiz — 147

Time to Say Goodbye — 148
Awards — 149
Count Your Flex Coins — 152
Check Your Answers — 153
Acknowledgments — 154
References — 156

Foreword

If you're a kid reading this foreword, stop!!! It's really boring!!! Skip this bit, and go to chapter 1, where the fun stuff begins.

If you're a parent or a therapist reading this foreword—well, to be perfectly honest, the same advice applies to you, because the rest of the book is vastly more interesting, enjoyable, and useful than anything I have to say. But, hey, if you're determined to keep reading, I'll keep it brief.

Basically, you have in your hands (or on your device) a life-changing book for kids. Anna Scetinina has taken the scientifically proven model of acceptance and commitment therapy (ACT) and, with a great combination of humor, playfulness, and artistic talent, has turned it into a fun, practical, and easy-to-do program for helping kids transform their relationship with worry. (Confession: As someone who has made a career out of making ACT accessible for a public audience, I felt pangs of envy when I saw just how masterfully Anna has achieved this.)

Packed full of creative, playful exercises for developing powerful new psychological skills, this book will help kids handle painful emotions effectively, unhook from their worries, act courageously, develop resilience, focus on what's important, engage in what they do, and realize their full potential. Given that all kids worry, this book is an invaluable resource for all parents and caregivers, as well as an essential tool for any therapist.

So, please don't waste any more of your valuable time reading this foreword. Instead, get into the interesting stuff!

Good luck and have fun as you go!

RUSS HARRIS
Author of *The Happiness Trap* and *ACT Made Simple*

A Letter to Parents

If you are reading this book, most likely you know a child who struggles with worry, and you are looking for solutions. Well, I have good and bad news. The bad news is that this workbook will not cure your child of worry. Feeling anxious sometimes is normal. The good news is the book will help your child develop a flexible mindset to cope with their worry effectively. Moreover, the skills your child will learn will help them deal much better with other difficult feelings, such as anger, sadness, and disappointment. Maybe better than you can deal with your own difficult feelings. Perhaps your child will even teach you some helpful skills as they go through the activities.

How ACT can help

The book uses acceptance and commitment therapy (ACT). ACT is an evidence-based therapy that helps people develop psychological flexibility, live more meaningfully, and successfully cope with emotions and stressors. ACT has been proven effective for children who struggle with different types of worry (Hancock et al. 2016). In this book, I adapt ACT principles to children's developmental level using simple language, engaging activities, illustrations, and fun characters to help them grasp the ideas. My vision was to create a type of book that a child would want to work in and go back to whenever they need.

How to support your child in reading and doing the activities

Introducing this book to your child is an essential first step in assisting them to succeed in developing coping skills and a flexible mindset. This book is designed for children ages 5 to 12 to read independently or with the guidance of a trusted adult. Most kids can navigate this book alone. Younger children, those who aren't enthusiastic about reading, or those who may be hesitant to use a self-help book will benefit from some initial help. Flip through the book together, discuss the characters, and try out a few activities to pique your child's interest and encourage them to give it a go. The additional benefit is that you'll become familiar with the tools and can assist your child when they struggle with their worries.

To motivate your child, the book has something to incentivize their engagement. After each section, your child will do a quiz to reinforce what they learned. For every correct answer, they will earn a flex coin. A *flex coin* is a token to reward them for learning new skills, with a maximum of five per quiz. At the end of the book, they will receive a special award with an honorary title. The title will be determined by the number of coins collected.

To boost your child's motivation and commitment to doing the activities, you may introduce rewards based on the number of coins your child gets in each of the seven sections. Rewarding your child's effort with a meaningful shared experience is best. For example, play a game together, go for ice cream, or watch a movie. You can also offer small rewards, such as stickers, to support your child's focus and engagement. Having a smaller reward after each section and a bigger reward upon completion of the book tends to work best.

Help your child get organized

To maximize the benefits of this book, I highly recommend following the chronological order of the sections. Each section builds upon the knowledge gained in the previous one, so please encourage your child to complete the activities in sequence.

Before your child begins, I also suggest downloading the PDF and audio files available at *http://www.newharbinger.com/53424*. These include copies of all the quizzes and materials for some activities. If your child wishes to retake a quiz, for example, you can help them reprint it. Audio files are available for some activities, which can help your child's engagement and enjoyment. The following icons indicate if an activity has an audio component or a printable element:

For each activity, your child will need a pen or pencil and an assortment of colored markers or crayons. Additionally, several activities call for collecting some household objects. You will notice that almost every activity provides lines for written responses. However, if your child feels more comfortable expressing themselves through drawings, provide them with blank sheets of paper.

Thank you for your trust and the opportunity to help support your child in coping with their worries effectively. I hope they will have a great time reading the book and doing the activities.

—**Anna**

A Note for Professionals

Acceptance and commitment therapy (ACT) has been proven effective for a broad range of concerns, including anxiety disorders (Gloster et al. 2020). Studies have shown that using ACT leads to significant improvements in child psychological functioning and reduction of anxiety symptoms as well as reduction of parental stress (Byrne et al. 2020; Fang and Ding 2020; Hancock et al. 2016). Research has also demonstrated that young children can grasp ACT concepts successfully (Hancock et al. 2016). If you are an ACT professional working with kids ages 5 to 12 who are struggling with different types of anxiety, worry, and stress, you may find adapting and implementing ACT a bit challenging with this age group, especially if you do online therapy.

The activities in this book and free downloadable PDF and audio files, available at *http://www.newharbinger.com/53424*, can help support your work with younger clients, making therapy more exciting and engaging during sessions and in between. These include copies of all the quizzes, some activity templates, and audio files for mindfulness practices. The following icons indicate if an activity has an audio component or a printable element:

The workbook's structure

The first section of this workbook provides psychoeducation on worry and anxiety. (Note: In this book, I use the word worry interchangeably with the word anxiety to describe the feeling and cognitive process.) Children's psychological flexibility is evaluated using a questionnaire adapted from the Acceptance and Fusion Questionnaire for Youth (AFQ-Y8) by Greco, Lambert, and Baer (2008).

The ACT Hexaflex model is presented in section 2 as the "Flex Park," where different attractions represent the six core ACT processes of psychological change. As children visit various parts of the Flex Park throughout the book, they learn ACT skills and strategies and develop a more flexible mindset.

Sections 3 to 6 cover the processes of acceptance, defusion, self-as-context, mindfulness, and values. Section 7 focuses on the process of committed action and introduces kids to self-compassion. At the end of the book, psychological flexibility is reevaluated to measure the changes.

Make it fun

As an ACT therapist, I use visuals and draw in sessions to make activities fun and metaphors memorable. When I ask my young clients and their parents what they remember from the previous session, they often say "the image you showed" or "the picture you drew." I hope that activities, illustrations, toolboxes with strategies, printable copies of some activities, and the audio files from this book will help you in doing ACT with your young clients in an engaging and effective way.

—Anna

A Letter to Kids

My name is Anna. I am a therapist. I help kids and adults deal with difficult feelings and thoughts. Just like your doctor helps you keep your body healthy, I help kids keep their minds healthy. I wrote and drew the art in this book to help you cope with your worries better!

This is a self-help book. Do you know what that means? It means you read it and do fun activities by yourself. You can also read it with a parent or sibling if you'd like. If you need help understanding any of the ideas, you can always ask an adult you trust to help.

This book is based on a way of helping people called acceptance and commitment therapy (ACT for short). *Acceptance* means letting feelings and thoughts be. *Commitment* means doing things that make life better. *Therapy* means learning tools and skills to cope with difficult feelings with the help of a health care professional.

ACT teaches you how to:

- stay focused on what's happening now
- accept things you can't control
- create an exciting life
- take brave actions

The activities in this book will help you develop what I call a *flexible mindset*. Sound a bit confusing? Sure, let me explain. A *mindset* is basically how you tend to think about things. The activities in this book will help you become more flexible in your thinking. When you're *flexible* in thinking, you're willing to try new things even when it is hard! It also gets easier to deal with strong feelings, like worry. In other words, developing a flexible mindset is like training your brain muscles.

Do you like to play? Of course, who doesn't? Then I have good news. This book teaches fun ways to deal with your worries. My team of helpers makes it even better. Let's meet them.

Worry monsters keep you company when you read the book. They also help explain ideas.

Brainy shares lots of cool facts about science.

Curious Cat practices different activities with you.

Mighty Mouse loves playing hide-and-seek. See if you can find her on every page!

As you learn, you will earn special coins. I call them flex coins. After you read the book and do the activities, you can use your flex coins to get a special award. The more coins you earn, the better! Keep track of your flex coins on page 152.

Did I get you excited? Awesome. Then grab a pencil or a pen, crayons or markers, and some paper. Let's start section 1.

—Anna

What You Will Learn

In section 1, you will:

- Learn about different types of worries and different types of worriers
- Notice how worry feels in your body
- Discover why you worry
- See how flexible your mind is
- Think about things you do to feel safe when worry comes

Ready to start? Great! Let's begin.

 This picture means that the activity has a file you can print. To get the files, go to *http://www.newharbinger.com/53424*.

Section 1

Understanding Your Worry

☐ Do you ever have thoughts that make you feel upset or worried?
☐ Do these thoughts happen often, even when you don't want them to?
☐ Do you sometimes have trouble falling asleep because you're worried?

If you said yes to any of these questions, you may be worrying too much. It's okay to worry sometimes (everyone does). But worrying too much can make life difficult. Worrying can take up a lot of time. It can also stop you from trying new things, doing important things, and having fun.

Look at the worry monsters and check out what they worry about. Do you worry about any of these things too?

Color and name these worry monsters.

1

ACTIVITY 1

Are You a Worrier?

What do you worry about? Kids worry about a lot of things. I listed some of those things below. Put a check mark next to those that you worry about.

- ☐ Doing your homework right
- ☐ Being late to school
- ☐ Getting a bad grade
- ☐ Taking a test
- ☐ Changing schools
- ☐ Leaving the house
- ☐ Being away from your parents
- ☐ Being alone
- ☐ Being different than others
- ☐ Feeling embarrassed
- ☐ Feeling judged
- ☐ Making new friends
- ☐ Talking to people
- ☐ Bullies

- ☐ Germs
- ☐ Chemicals
- ☐ Doctors
- ☐ Needles
- ☐ Animals
- ☐ Insects
- ☐ Robbers
- ☐ Darkness
- ☐ Being too high up
- ☐ Thunder
- ☐ Lightning
- ☐ Asking for help
- ☐ Monsters under the bed
- ☐ Broccoli for dinner

Write down anything else that worries you.

_____

_____

COOL FACTS

Did you know you are more likely to be a worrier if your parents or grandparents worry a lot?

Types of Worriers

When you worry a lot, you turn into a worrier. You start thinking about bad or scary things that might happen. Worrying can also stop you from doing fun things. Here are some different types of worriers. Are you like one of these types? After you read about the different types, make up your own type.

Always-Worried Worrier

Job: Stays alert for danger all the time
Hobby: Thinks about scary things day and night
Energy level: Very tired
Superpower: Knows how to get comforted by a parent

Shy Worrier

Job: Thinks a lot about what others think
Hobby: Skips school when possible
Energy level: Exhausted
Superpower: Mind-reading

Space Worrier

Job: Avoids places (malls, movie theaters, elevators)
Hobby: Clings to parent
Energy level: Overworked
Superpower: Knows best ways to escape

"What-If?" Worrier

Job: Scared of germs, robbers, and mistakes
Hobby: Washes hands, checks locks, does homework over and over again
Energy level: Drained
Superpower: Wonderful imagination

Natural Worrier

Job: Watches for spiders, snakes, and storms
Hobby: Stays at home
Energy level: On alert
Superpower: Great at checking surroundings and weather reports

_____ Worrier

Job: _____

Hobby: _____

Energy level: _____

Superpower: _____

WHAT YOU LEARNED

I worry about _____

ACTIVITY 2

Where Do You Feel Worry in Your Body?

How does your body feel when you are worried about doing something new or hard? Like going to a new class, trying a new sport, or going on a plane for the first time? Your heart may start beating faster. Your muscles might get tight. You might feel hot or cold, or even shaky. It is normal to feel this way when you're doing something new or hard and don't know if it will go okay. It's the way your body is keeping you safe.

COOL FACTS

When you feel worried, your tummy might feel funny. And you might need to go to the bathroom more! It's because the part of your body that processes food slows down when you worry. Everything will go back to normal when worry passes.

My eyes get huge. My fur stands up. My tail gets furry. My ears lie flat!

Worry in My Body

Think about all the changes in your body when you worry.

- To answer the questions on the next page, circle words that tell how you feel. There's a line where you can add words, if you'd like.

- Color in the parts of your body on the next page to show where you feel worry.

How do your arms and legs feel?
Cold, hot, tingly, heavy, frozen, shaky,

How does your head feel?
Heavy, tight, achy,

How does your skin look?
Lighter than usual, blushed, like it has spots,

How does your heart feel and sound?
Loud, pounding, fast, slow,

How does your belly feel?
Burning, twisted, heavy, like it has butterflies in it,

How do your body and muscles feel?
Stiff, nervous, tight, shaky,

How do your eyes look and feel?
Teary, moving fast, tight,

How does your jaw feel?
Tight, shaky,

Where does your worry usually start? If you remember, mark that part of the body drawing with a star.

WHAT YOU LEARNED

When I worry, my _____

Now you know a bit more about how your body reacts to worry. Do you want to know why it reacts that way? Turn the page.

5

ACTIVITY 3

Your Brain's Main Job

Let's go back 200,000 years ago and visit some friendly cave people. Back then, there were many dangers and people worried about lots of things. Look at the pictures below and circle things that you think cave people worried about. Check your answers at the bottom of the page.

Use the answers to fill in the blanks in the story below.

Long Ago

Long ago, people lived in caves. They hunted to find food and built 1. _____ to keep warm at night. They feared 2. _____, like bears and wolves. 3. _____ scared them because lightning could set fires to their homes. To help keep each other safe, they lived in groups and were afraid of 4. _____. The more they could protect themselves from danger, the longer they lived. So, they were always on the lookout for danger.

When cave people were in danger, their brains would get their bodies ready to do something about it. Their brains prepared their bodies to fight, run away from, or not be noticed by what scared them. This response is called the *fight-flight-or-freeze response*.

Answers: 1. fires, 2. animals, 3. storms, 4. unfriendly cave people

6

Fight-Flight-or-Freeze Response

Dangers are different today. You don't need to save yourself from wild animals, and you can stay home during storms. But your brain still reacts the same way it did long ago to anything it thinks is a danger. When something makes you scared or worried, your brain gets your body ready to fight, run away, or freeze in place. It tries to protect you because keeping you safe is your brain's main job.

Let's talk about what it feels like when your body wants you to fight, flight, or freeze.

Fight	Flight	Freeze
What you think: I can win against this danger!	**What you think:** I can't beat this danger. I need to run away!	**What you think:** I can't fight the danger, and I can't get away!
What your body does: It gives you extra energy to fight. You may feel angry, your heart beats fast, you feel hot, and your belly is burning. You may sweat more, make fists, or tighten muscles.	**What your body does:** You may feel like you can't stay still. Your eyes may get wider or tear up. You may feel sick to your stomach. You feel like you want to hide away. You may even throw up!	**What your body does:** It helps you stop moving and freeze in place. If you don't move, maybe no one will see you! Your skin may get lighter and colder. You may not see clearly and feel like it's hard to speak. You may hold your breath. You feel terrified.

Color the monster that shows how you often feel when you're scared or worried.

WHAT YOU LEARNED

When I worry, my brain gets my body to _____

_____ to keep me safe.

ACTIVITY 4
Old Mind and New Mind

In this activity, you will check out how the brain tried to protect Homy, a cave kid, a long time ago. And you will compare it to how your brain tries to help you be safe in our time. Color the drawings and add your examples in blank spaces.

There might be a snake.

The teacher will be mad at me because I am late.

Saber-toothed tigers live here. I must stay away.

I lost the last race. I'm not trying again.

Do they like me?

Are they talking about me?

This road looks hard. I better not go down it.

This wall is tall. I could fall. I better not climb it.

What if they attack? I need to get away from here.

COOL FACTS

When you are scared, your brain makes a chemical called *adrenaline*. Adrenaline helps your body react more quickly. You breathe faster. Your heart beats faster. Your muscles get tight to help you run away from danger or fight it if you can. Your eyes get wider, so you can see better. This is like a superpower that helps you stay safe.

Keeping you safe is your brain's main job. It does not feel good when your brain prepares you to fight, run away, or freeze when you are scared. But your brain does this to help keep you safe. . . . Wait a minute! Where'd that mouse go?

WHAT YOU LEARNED

My brain is always on the lookout for _____ to keep me safe.

Now you know why your body acts a certain way when you get worried. In the next activity, you will check how flexible your mind is.

ACTIVITY 5

Do You Have a Flexible Mindset?

Remember when we talked about how having a flexible mindset can help deal better with worry? In this activity, you check how flexible your mind is. Follow these steps:

1. Read each sentence below. Think about how true you think it is.

2. Circle the number of points that best match how true the idea is for you.

3. Add up the total points in each column. Write the totals at the bottom.

	Not at all true	Pretty true	True	Very true
Worry makes my life hard.	3	2	1	0
I wish I had a magic wand to make my worries disappear.	3	2	1	0
To have a good life, I need to get rid of my worries and fears.	3	2	1	0
If I worry, that means the bad thing will happen.	3	2	1	0
I always try to get rid of bad thoughts and feelings.	3	2	1	0
Worrying is terrible. I can't stand it.	3	2	1	0
I am afraid of trying new things.	3	2	1	0
When I worry, I don't do things that are important to me.	3	2	1	0
When I worry, I do worse at school.	3	2	1	0
If I worry, something must be wrong with me.	3	2	1	0

Until worry goes away, I can't make friends.	3	2	1	0
Until fear goes away, I can't try new things.	3	2	1	0
I worry a lot about what others think of me.	3	2	1	0
Total points				

 Each point earns you one flex coin. Add your total to the Count Your Flex Coins chart on page 152. You'll also repeat this activity at the end of the book. If you've become more flexible in your thinking after doing work in this book, you will likely score more points.

WHAT YOU LEARNED

I earned _____ points. It is very true, that _____

I got _____ flex coins. It is not at all true, that _____

Good job! In the next activity, you will look at what worry can make you do.

ACTIVITY 6

What Do You Do When You Worry?

When you worry that something won't go well, you might avoid doing that thing. You may also try to make sure your fear will not come true. And you might do things that make you feel safer. For example, if you are scared of bugs, you may avoid going outside. You may also choose to not ride your bike or go on a walk with friends. And when your family has a picnic in the backyard, you may decide to hide in your room.

Different people do different things to deal with their worries. Here are some more examples.

Safe and Sound

WORRY THOUGHTS	WORRY ACTIONS
I am not going to hike because there could be spiders. Spiders can bite and they are so disgusting!	• avoid going outside • check for spiders in the house • wear clothes that cover my arms and legs
Is there going to be a storm? Thunder is so scary. It makes my heart beat faster!	• ask Mom or Dad to stay nearby • keep lights on • check weather reports • try to keep busy to not think of the storm
I touched the doorknob. Now there are germs on my hands! My hands feel dirty. I can get sick from germs!	• wash hands many times • sanitize hands and doorknobs • avoid touching doorknobs • open doors with a foot • change clothes several times a day

COOL FACTS

A *phobia* is a fear of something. Did you know that lots of people are afraid of spiders? The Greek word *arachne* means spider, so the fear of spiders is called *arachnophobia*. This is one of the most common fears. Also, many people are afraid of thunder and lightning. And even animals, such as dogs and cats, are sometimes afraid of that too. That fear is called *astraphobia*.

I have **as-tra-pho-bi-a.** I hate storms!

WORRY THOUGHTS	WORRY ACTIONS
What if I'm at school and don't know what to talk about with other kids? I will look silly.	• stay quiet • avoid making eye contact • pretend to read a book • check phone • avoid clothes in bright colors so I don't draw attention
What if I fail the test? My parents will be very upset with me. Everyone will think I am stupid.	• study for test for hours • wear "lucky" clothes • check test answers again and again
What if nobody wants to play with me at the birthday party? I will be standing alone all the time.	• avoid going to the party • go to the party but avoid talking to kids • cling to Mom or Dad • try to not be noticed

Now, what do you do when your worry shows up? Are there things you avoid doing when you worry? Are there things you do to make yourself feel safer? Write some examples.

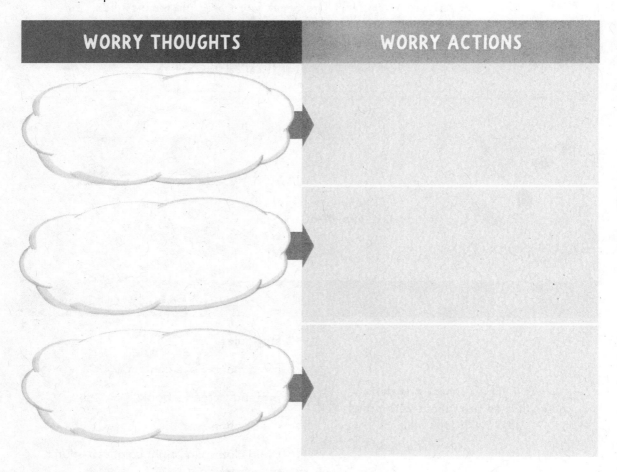

Avoiding scary things or doing things that make you feel safer can make you feel better right away. That makes you want to do those things again and again. But worry always comes back, right? This is something we're going to talk more about.

WHAT YOU LEARNED

When I have worry thoughts, I _____

You made it to the end of the section 1. Congrats! In section 2, you will learn more about developing a flexible mindset.

Section 1 Quiz

Answer the quiz questions below to collect more flex coins. Circle the letter you think is the right answer.

1. **Worrying too much**
   a) helps me prepare for the worst
   b) can stop me from doing fun things
   c) helps me avoid danger

2. **When I worry, my heart starts beating faster. This is**
   a) a sign that there is something wrong with me
   b) a normal reaction, my body is trying to protect me
   c) dangerous and I must tell my parents about this right away

3. **My brain's main job is to**
   a) give me something to worry about
   b) remind me of all the dangerous things
   c) keep me safe

4. **Responses to danger are called**
   a) fight
   b) flight
   c) freeze
   d) all of the above

5. **When I worry, I may start**
   a) doing things that make me feel safe
   b) avoid important things
   c) miss out on exciting activities
   d) all of the above

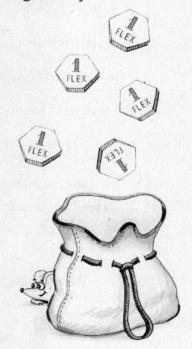

Great job on doing your first quiz! Each correct answer earns one flex coin. On this page, color the number of coins that you got yellow. Add your total to page 152.

If you missed an answer, look back at the activity that talked about the topic. If you want to take the quiz again, ask a parent to print out a copy.

Answers: 1. b, 2. b, 3. c, 4. d, 5. d

What You Will Learn

In section 2, you will:

- Start exploring the Flex Park
- Learn more about how a flexible mindset can help you deal with your worries
- Practice choosing the Toward Road
- Travel into the future and set goals to work on
- Make a thermometer that measures your feelings
- Fill out your feelings journal

Ready to keep going? Then read on.

 This picture means that the activity has a file you can print. To get the files, go to *http://www.newharbinger.com/53424*.

How to Grow a Flexible Mindset

I got you a ticket to the Flex Park! It is like an amusement park that has different fun attractions. Each attraction in this park teaches you skills that will help you develop a flexible mindset and deal with worry better. Get your crayons and markers ready to color the park attractions on the next page. You can color them now or color each one as you learn more about it in the book.

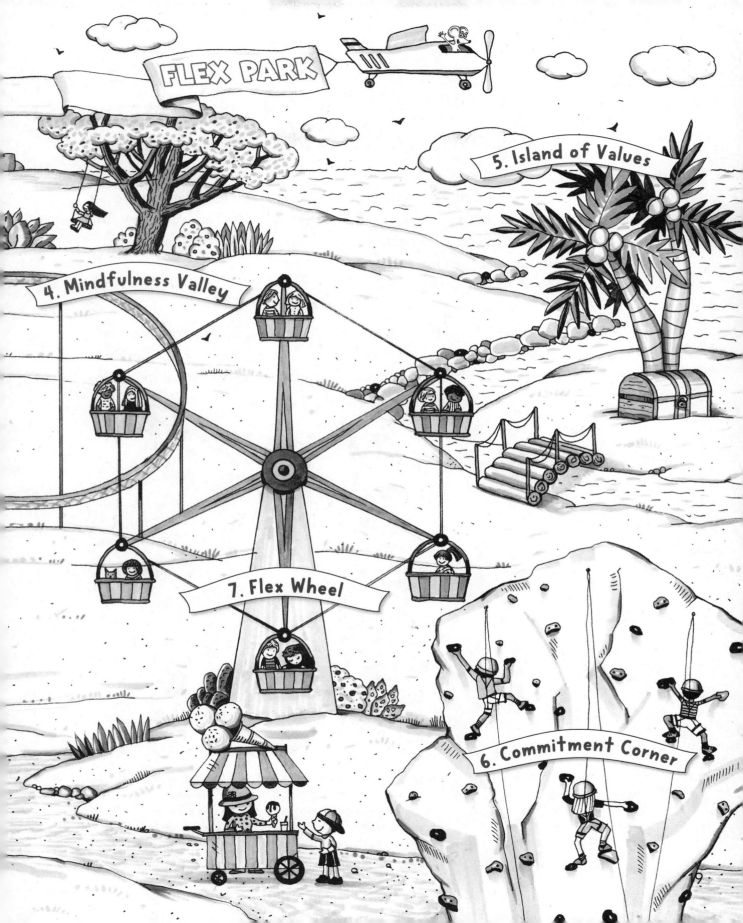

ACTIVITY 7

Flex Park Attractions and a Flexible Mindset

Do you want to know a bit more about the attractions of the Flex Park on the previous pages? Good, this is what you will do in this activity. This will help you better navigate the book and understand where we will go next. You also will learn more about having a flexible mindset.

Can You Guess?

Here is a fun task for you. Read the details below. Find each of these pictures on the Flex Park drawing on the previous pages. Then write the attraction's number in the circle on the matching picture. Check your answers at the bottom of the page.

You learn to stay focused on the present moment here.

You practice accepting difficult feelings here.

You look at what is important to you and what makes you happy here.

You learn how to take power off your worry thoughts here. That means your thoughts do not seem as scary anymore!

You practice paying attention to your feelings and thoughts without being caught up in worry here.

You act bravely and do important things, even when they are hard, here. And you become more confident that you can do hard things.

Answers from left to right. Top row: 4, 1, 5. Bottom row: 2, 3, 6

When you visit all of these areas of the Flex Park, you will

DEVELOP
your FLEXIBLE MINDSET by:

- Using skills you learned to **accept** things you can't control, like difficult thoughts, feelings, and memories
- Discovering how to **create** a life that's fun and exciting
- Choosing to **take brave actions**, like facing your fears, reaching your goals, and standing up to new challenges

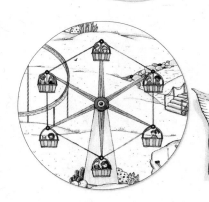

You can then hop on the Flex Wheel and deal with your worries with confidence. Remember this ACT formula:

ACCEPT + CREATE + TAKE ACTION = FLEXIBLE MINDSET

COOL FACTS

Did you know why our brains have wrinkles on the outside? As people became smarter, our brains grew bigger. To fit inside our heads, they had to fold themselves up. If the brain could be smoothed out flat, it would be as big as a carpet!

Superhero

When you have a flexible mindset, you do things even when they're hard. You become like a superhero. On the next page, draw yourself as a superhero.

21

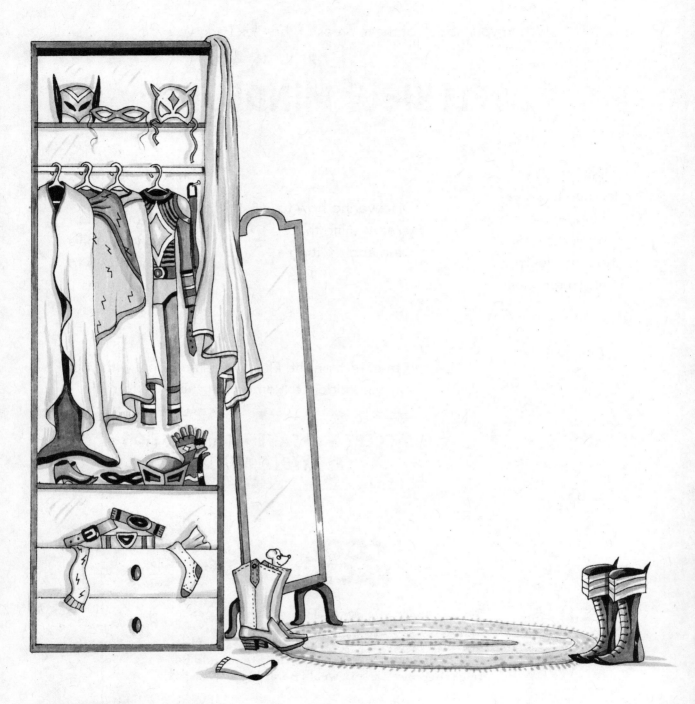

WHAT YOU LEARNED

If I have a flexible mindset, I can _____

_____

Word Search

ACTIVITY 8

Below I've hidden 12 words or sets of words about flexible mindsets and the Flex Park. Put your detective skills to the test. See if you can find them all. Check your answers at the end of the book.

```
C E B C W K E M G D S C V N A F F B
A Q U N H O O K I N G Y D J C Q Q K
T Q N H E I E H X N Q N I N C C H V
P U E P N B F E K H D R O V E R X A
C O M M I T M E N T N F N G P E K L
P T I L I B O L N B R U I T A E U
K H A C T X D P W U R O L L A T K E
U A C C E P T V Q D E G I U N E F S
O B S E R V A T I O N O U P C E E J
V F L E X I B L E M I N D S E T S G
X K N O L X H T A K E A C T I O N S
H G V F F L E X P A R K Y R L X L H
```

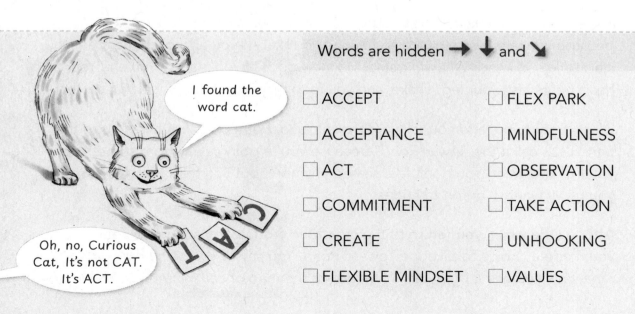

Words are hidden → ↓ and ↘

☐ ACCEPT
☐ ACCEPTANCE
☐ ACT
☐ COMMITMENT
☐ CREATE
☐ FLEXIBLE MINDSET
☐ FLEX PARK
☐ MINDFULNESS
☐ OBSERVATION
☐ TAKE ACTION
☐ UNHOOKING
☐ VALUES

23

Toward and Away Roads

Worry can make it hard to do things, like focus on your homework, try a new activity, or go to a friend's house. When you worry, you might stop paying attention in class, not hear what your parents say, and miss your friends' jokes. It is as if worry gets you like a fish on a hook!

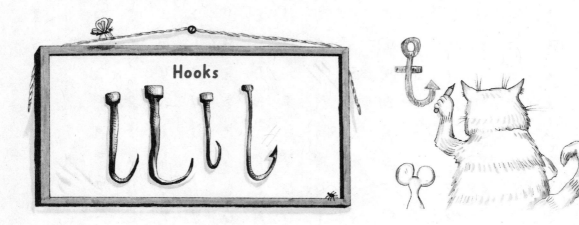

Choosing the Road

Imagine going to a special place, like the Flex Park, to meet your friends, go on the rides, and get ice cream. You are super excited!

To get there, you take a road through the woods. Let's call it *"Toward Road"* because you're moving toward something you like. As you approach the road, you start to feel worried. *What if I get lost in the woods? It looks scary in there!* Your heart beats fast, your legs shake, and you feel dizzy. You think, *Better not go there!*

Worry hooks you, and you take a different road. But it does not take you to the park. Let's call it the *"Away Road"* because you're going away from something you like and want. You don't feel scared anymore, but you miss your friends, and you really want to go on the rides!

After a little while, you return to the crossroad. Your worry shows up again, but you made a choice to take the Toward Road. You say to yourself, *I may get lost, or I may not get lost. If I get lost, I can look at the map or call my friends.* You notice that worry is still there. As you go, you also notice many interesting things. Can you find and circle eight cool things in the picture?

You make it to the Flex Park and have a wonderful day. You feel very proud of yourself for the choice you made!

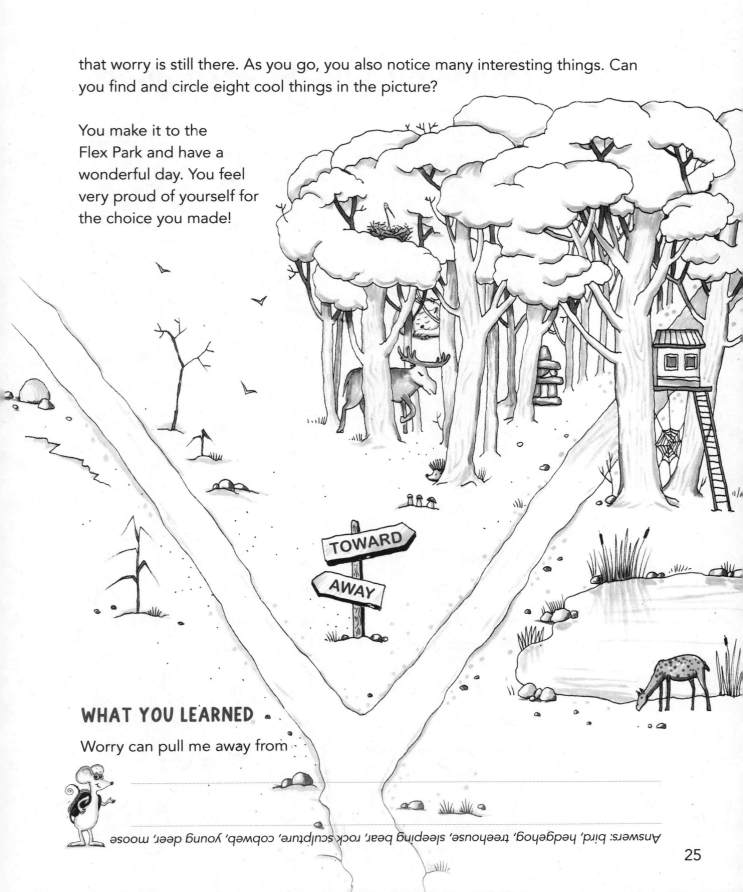

WHAT YOU LEARNED

Worry can pull me away from _____

Answers: bird, hedgehog, treehouse, sleeping bear, rock sculpture, cobweb, young deer, moose

25

ACTIVITY 10: Choosing the Toward Road

Did you notice that usually the things you worry about end up not being as scary as your mind tells you they are? If you keep going toward things that are important to you, even though worry is there, you feel proud of yourself. And each time you get more confident that you can do hard things!

Here is an example. Imagine you are worried about a test at school. If you let the worry thoughts hook you, you might spend a lot of time thinking about all the things that could go wrong. You will likely end up feeling very nervous. And it will be difficult to study. If, despite your worries, you study well and take the test, you will feel proud of yourself for all your hard work and for doing what you can.

Your Turn

Think of a situation that makes you worry.

What is happening? _____

How do you feel? _____

What do you think? _____

Read the questions below. Write your answers in the diagram on the next page. Make sure to match the question and answer numbers.

1. What could you do if worry hooks you?
2. What will you miss out on?
3. If you unhook from your worry, what can you do?
4. Why is that important?

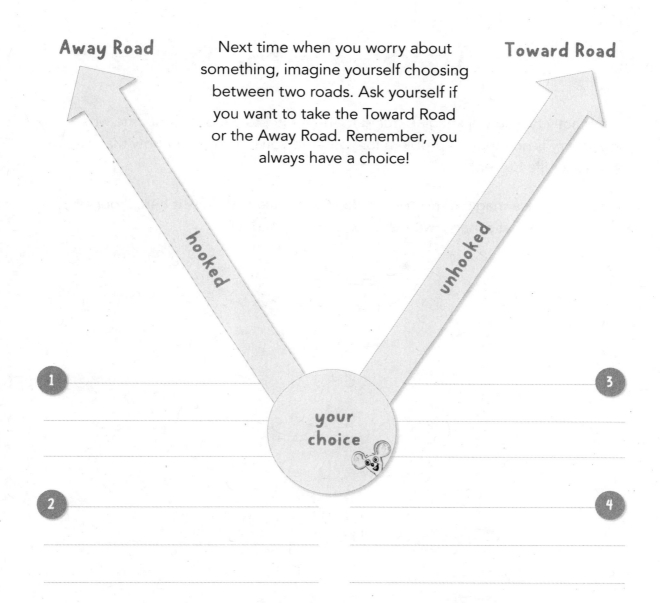

Next time when you worry about something, imagine yourself choosing between two roads. Ask yourself if you want to take the Toward Road or the Away Road. Remember, you always have a choice!

WHAT YOU LEARNED

When I am afraid, I may want to take the _____ Road. But I have a choice. I can instead take the _____ Road and do things that are hard but important to me.

In the following activities, you will learn how unhooking from your worry can help you choose the Toward Road more often. But first, you will practice some magic. Excited? Turn the page.

Travel into the Future

In this activity, you will imagine going to the future, to a moment of time when your worry is no longer a problem for you. And you'll think about how that will make your life better.

1. Imagine a magic wand you would like to have and draw it here. Look at Curious Cat's magic wands for wand design ideas.

Why did Mighty Mouse use a magic spell to travel to the future? She wanted to know if you found her on all the pages of this book!

2 Come up with a magic spell that can take you into the future. Write your spell here.

_____

_____

3 Use your magic wand, spell, and imagination to get to a time when your worries disappear. Draw or write on the clouds below how your life will be better when your worries are not a problem anymore.

What will you stop doing?

What will you start doing?

What will you do more often?

What new things will you try?

What will you do differently at school?

What will you do differently at home?

What will you do differently with friends?

29

Stairs of Importance

1 Think of five things you can do differently in the future, when you develop a more flexible mindset and learn to deal with your worry better. Write these things on the steps of the ladder below.

2 In the circle next to each step, rate how important each thing is to you. Use numbers from 1 to 5, where 1 is the most important and 5 is the least important. These are your goals for change.

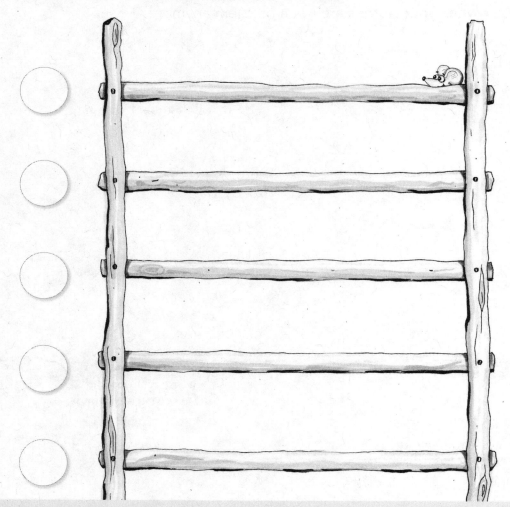

WHAT YOU LEARNED

When my worry is no longer a problem, I will be able to _____

30

End Goals Versus Action Goals

ACTIVITY 12

There are two types of goals you can set for yourself:

- *End goals* are things you want to get or to have. But they aren't fully in your control.

- *Action goals* are things you can do to make it more likely to reach your end goals.

COOL FACTS

Did you know that setting goals helps you be more successful in life? This is because you focus your attention on your goal, put effort into reaching it, and keep trying. Reaching goals also makes you feel good about your ability to get things done!

Look at the goals below. Decide which ones are end goals and which ones are action goals. Sort them on the board on the next page.

1. Win the basketball game.
2. Practice basketball for an hour every day.
3. Attend every soccer practice and work on improving skills.
4. Get an A on the math test.
5. Make the soccer team.
6. Study for the math test for 30 minutes each day.
7. Pick my science fair project and get books to read.
8. Get a trophy in the science fair.

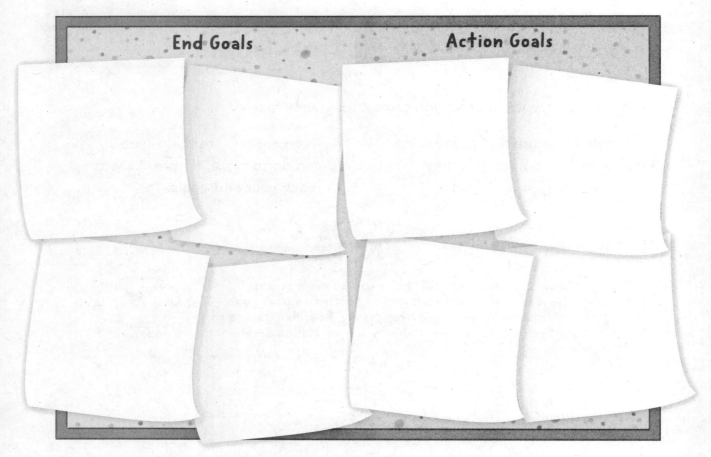

Now, check the goals on your stairs of importance on page 30. Are there some end goals that are not fully in your control? Change them into action goals and write these new goals below.

_____

_____

WHAT YOU LEARNED

Action goal means _____

_____

Great job. Now, get your markers ready for the next activity.

Answers: Action goals 2, 3, 6, 7; End goals 1, 4, 5, 8

Your Feelings Thermometer

ACTIVITY 13

You probably noticed that your worry is not always the same. It may feel a bit like a roller coaster. Sometimes, it's very big and scary. Other times, it is just like a little bump in the road.

In this activity, you will draw what's called the **feelings thermometer**. It will help you measure how strong your feelings are. You can use it for some other things too, like how important something is to you. The thermometer goes from 1 (very low) to 10 (very high).

Draw a picture of a thermometer in the space below. Write the numbers 1 through 10 up the side of the thermometer, with 1 at the bottom and 10 at the top. Try to space the numbers so they're about the same distance apart.

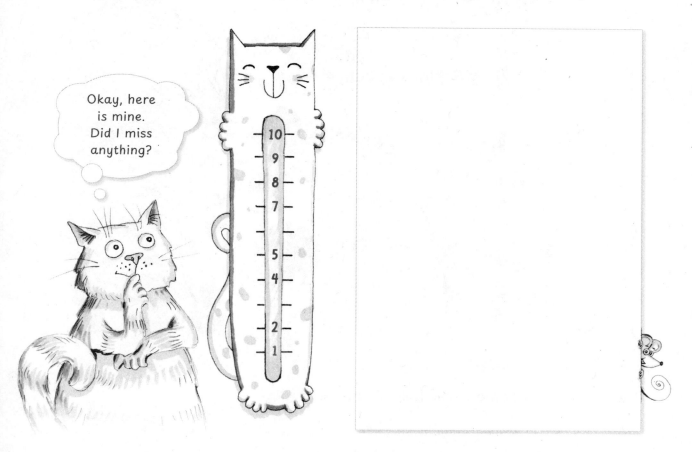

Worries Come in Different Sizes

Look at these pictures of worry monsters below. They are worried, but each one is worried in a different way. Using your feelings thermometer, decide how big the worry is for each monster. Write the number in the circle beside each monster. So, write the number 1 if the worry monster is only a little worried. Write the number 10 if you think the worry monster is really, really worried.

WHAT YOU LEARNED

The feelings thermometer can help me measure _____

_____

My Worry Is Like...

ACTIVITY 14

In this activity, you compare your worries to a thing that's like them.

When you describe something by comparing it to something else, you can help other people understand it better.

Yes, Curious Cat. You are right. When you say something is "light as a feather," you're not saying that the thing you're describing is a feather. You're comparing it to a feather, which weighs very little.

What do worries feel like to you? Here are some examples to get you thinking.

- *My worries are like a roller coaster. They can be scary. But just like the ride will end, my worries will go away in time.*

- *My worries are like clouds in the sky. Some are big and dark. Others are small and fluffy. But just like clouds, my worries come and go.*

Your Turn

Now, finish this sentence by comparing your worries to something they are like.

" My worries are like _____

_____

_____

_____ "

In the next activity, you will practice looking at how your feelings change.

 # Notice How Your Feelings Change

Your last activity in this section of the book is about noticing and tracking how your feelings change during the day. You're going to spend a whole week paying attention and coloring in a journal. I bet that by the end of the week, you'll be a master at noticing how your feelings come and go. For this activity, use the "My Feelings Journal" form on the next page and follow these directions.

1. Pick a color or a symbol (or both) for each feeling named at the top of the form.

2. Pick a day to start paying attention to your feelings. You may begin today!

3. During each day, pay attention to how you feel. Try to notice your feelings in the morning, during the day, and in the evening. Do the best you can.

4. Each time you notice how you feel, color the square with the color you chose for that feeling or draw the symbol you picked.

5. Use your feelings thermometer to decide how strong the feeling is. Add a number from 1 (not strong at all) to 10 (really, really strong) to the square.

6. Keep going until you complete your whole journal form.

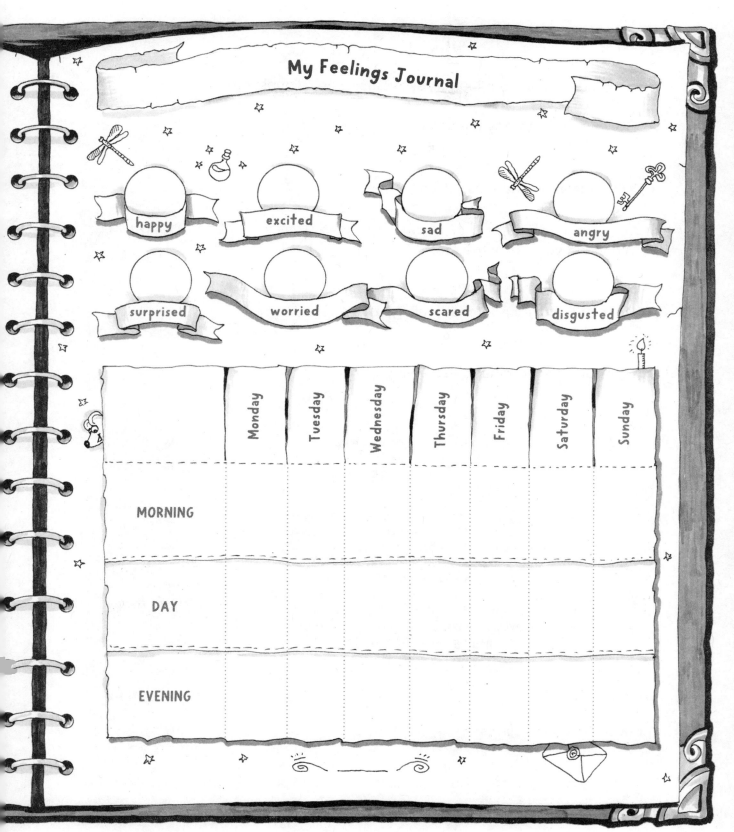

What Did You Notice?

Once you complete your journal, ask yourself these questions:

- Do your feelings stay the same during the day?

- What feeling came most often?

- When did you worry the most?

- How long did your hardest feeling last?

- How long did your happiest feeling last?

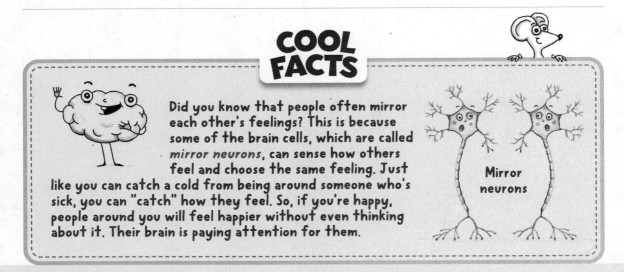

COOL FACTS

Did you know that people often mirror each other's feelings? This is because some of the brain cells, which are called *mirror neurons*, can sense how others feel and choose the same feeling. Just like you can catch a cold from being around someone who's sick, you can "catch" how they feel. So, if you're happy, people around you will feel happier without even thinking about it. Their brain is paying attention for them.

Mirror neurons

WHAT YOU LEARNED

I noticed that my feelings

It is time to do the section quiz and earn more flex coins. See how many flex coins you get this time!

Section 2 Quiz

1. You can develop a flexible mindset by:
   a) using skills you will learn in this book
   b) doing important things even when it is hard
   c) thinking positive thoughts
   d) both a) and b) are correct

2. When worry hooks you, you may
   a) spend a lot of time worrying
   b) get even more scared by thinking scary thoughts
   c) avoid doing things that are important or fun
   d) all of the above

3. Setting action goals helps you
   a) be successful and feel good about what you can do
   b) move toward your end goals
   c) know what you need to do to improve your skills
   d) all of the above

4. You can use the feelings thermometer
   a) to measure the temperature
   b) to decide how strong your feeling is
   c) to play

5. A difficult feeling
   a) will change like the weather
   b) will never go away
   c) is always very strong

Each correct answer earns one flex coin. On this page, color the number of coins that you got yellow. Add your total to page 152.

If you missed an answer, look back at the activity that talked about the topic. If you want to take the quiz again, ask a parent to print out a copy.

Answers: 1.d, 2.d, 3.d, 4.b, 5.a

What You Will Learn

In section 3, you will:

- Explore if you can feel one way and act in a different way
- Test if you can stop worrying
- Discover what makes worries bigger
- Take a few Acceptance Rides in the Flex Park
- Practice being curious about the way you feel
- Learn to let your worry be and make space for it
- Befriend your worry

You will also learn that your feelings carry a message for you. You get to decide what is best to do with this message. Ready to continue? Read on!

 This picture means that the activity has a file you can print. To get the files, go to *http://www.newharbinger.com/53424*.

Section 3

Befriend Your Worry

Have you ever played tug-of-war? It's a game where two teams pull on a rope to see who is stronger. Now imagine that you are playing tug-of-war against a worry monster on a big cliff. There is a deep pit between you and the monster. You're pulling on one end of the rope. The monster is pulling on the other end. The monster is trying to make you fall off the cliff. You try hard. But the monster is really big, scary, and strong. And it won't let go of the rope! The more you pull, the more it pulls back. What could you do? Write your thoughts on the lines below. Then keep reading. You will get to the answer at the end of section 3.

ACTIVITY 16

"Don't Worry"

Have you ever been told not to feel a certain way? Perhaps you were worried when going to a new place and your parents said, "Why do you worry? Nothing to worry about." Did that take the worry away? No? You probably still felt worried or maybe even annoyed. I would, too. You don't choose to worry in the first place, right?

Or maybe you were told to calm down or take your mind off worrying by doing things you enjoy. For example, reading a book, drawing, or playing a game. How did that work?

In the space below, draw or write things you have tried when you worry to calm yourself or put your mind off it. Then circle the ones that helped you feel better.

Some of the things you drew or wrote might help in the moment. But worry always come back, right?

COOL FACTS

Remember when we talked about your body's fight-flight-or-freeze response on page 7? That's how your body responds quickly to what your brain thinks is a danger. When you get scared by things you see, hear, smell, taste, or touch, your brain makes your body respond extremely fast. And your body can respond in the same way to just a scary thought, even though there is no actual danger nearby!

Your Turn

So, it seems like you can't make your worry stop or go away forever. But let's see if you can choose how you react to it. To do that, think of times when you feel one way, but act in a different way. Here are some examples:

- Wanting to stay in bed on rainy mornings but getting ready and going to school
- Being scared to go on a roller coaster but choosing to go with a friend
- Wanting to play with friends but finishing school homework first

Write some examples from your life:

_____

_____

_____

You might have noticed that you have a choice about how you respond to your difficult feelings. And as your examples show, you are already doing that. In the following activities, you will learn skills to help you act in a different way when you worry.

WHAT YOU LEARNED

I can feel _____

and act _____

You Can Stop Growing Worries

Worry feels bad. Of course, you want to win the tug-of-war game against worry and get rid of it. Who wouldn't? But trying to get rid of it can actually make things worse. Let me explain what I mean. When you worry, you may think, *Why do I always worry so much?* Thinking like that can make you angry. Then you may feel sad about feeling angry. Now you feel worried, angry, and sad. It's like your feelings grow and stack up like nesting dolls stacked inside each other. Here is another example:

Situation: Getting ready to talk in front of your class

What if I make a mistake? Everyone will laugh at me. → My heart beats so fast. I hate that! → Why do I always worry about things? → I can't focus now.

Worry → Anger → Sadness → Let down

45

If you get stuck on your worry, it tends to get bigger. And other unpleasant feelings may show up too! Then you may stop paying attention to important things.

In fact, you just missed four fun things hidden on the dolls! Look for them now.

COOL FACTS

When you try very hard to make your worry go away, your brain thinks the worry is bad and you are unsafe. And it protects you by keeping on your fight-flight-or-freeze response. And this makes you feel even more worried. So, the more you want your worry to go away, the longer your brain will keep this response on!

Your Turn

You're going to practice noticing how your worry grows. Follow the directions below using the nesting dolls on the next page.

1. Choose one of the examples below or think of your own:

   - [ ] You are taking a test, and you don't know the answer.
   - [ ] You're at a birthday party, and it is too loud.
   - [ ] You are going to a new class for the first time.
   - [ ] You are getting on a plane.
   - [ ] You don't want to get a shot because you're scared of needles.

2. Write a thought in each thought bubble above the dolls.

3. Write a matching feeling on each line under the dolls.

4. Draw the dolls' faces to show what they're feeling.

5. Color the dolls as you'd like.

Oh, wow! Beautiful work. Did your worry get bigger? What did you notice?

Answers: smiley face, banana, ghost, Mighty Mouse

Situation _____
_____

Thoughts

Feelings

WHAT YOU LEARNED

Worry can grow when I _____

Fighting worry or trying to make it stop does not work well. Do you want to try something new? Wonder what? Keep reading.

ACTIVITY 18

Meet Your Fear

It is time to go on the Acceptance Ride in the Flex Park to practice accepting your feelings. Here, you're not going to try to make your worry go away. You're going to notice it and look at it with curiosity. Letting the worry stay without trying to change it may feel a bit like a roller coaster.

But you will act bravely and trust that the ride is safe. I am sure you'll be proud of yourself for sticking with it! Curious Cat will help you.

Oh, no! I started to worry. I guess it's a good time to take the Acceptance Ride!

Describe Your Worry

Notice and describe what your worry feels like. What shape does it have? What color is it? How big is it?

It feels like a heavy yellow ball in my belly. The ball is rolling around. It feels like it has spikes. It's like a prickly melon!

COOL FACTS

 Did you know that eating lots of foods from nature, like colorful fruits, vegetables, and seeds, can help your mood? For example, prickly melon, a special type of melon that has spikes, has *magnesium* in it. Magnesium is a mineral that helps you feel calmer.

Your Turn

Think about a moment when you felt worried. What happened? Does thinking about it bring on some worry now? In the picture below, draw your worry and describe it like Curious Cat described his worry. When you are done, notice how the worry feels. Has anything changed?

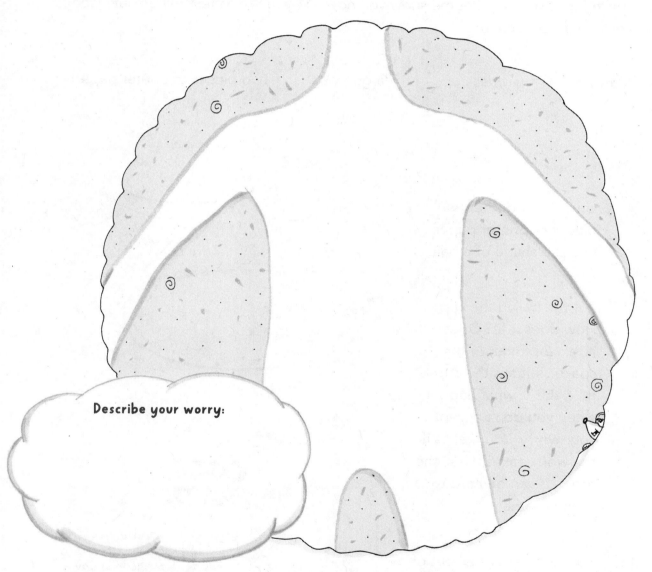

Describe your worry:

WHAT YOU LEARNED

When I notice my worry and describe it, giving it a shape and a color, it feels *easier / harder / the same* (circle one).

ACTIVITY 19

Make Room for Your Worry

Ready for another round on the Acceptance Ride? This time you learn to create space for your worry. Let me show you how. Do you like to test things out? Cool. Let's do an experiment.

Materials: ☐ small cup   ☐ large pot   ☐ two pieces of printer paper

Directions

1. Crumple together two pieces of printer paper into the shape of a ball.

2. Put the ball in the cup. How does it fit? Does it take up most of the space? If it fills the cup fully, this is what happens when you don't accept your worry. You feel as if the worry takes up all the room. It can be hard to even breathe!

3. Take the paper ball out of the cup. Put it in the large pot. Does it now have lots of space to roll around?

COOL FACTS

When you are little, you know and use only a few words to describe how you feel. As you grow, you learn many more feeling words. Getting better at describing different feelings helps you respond to them more easily.

50

When you make room for your worries, you handle them better. Imagine becoming super stretchy inside and giving your worry as much room as it needs. Look at the pictures below.

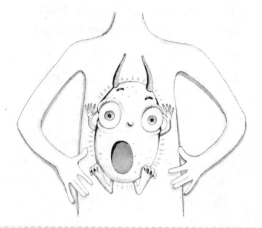

In the first picture, the worry monster takes up all the space. If you hold your worry tight, you may feel very scared and tense.

In the second picture, the worry monster has more room. As you imagine making space around your worry, you may feel less tense and uncomfortable. Your worry may not seem as scary anymore. It now has space to move, grow, or shrink until it goes away and a new feeling takes its place. When you make room for worry, it is also easier to notice many other things. Like where you are, who is around, and what you are doing. Then you can better choose what is more important in the moment than your worry.

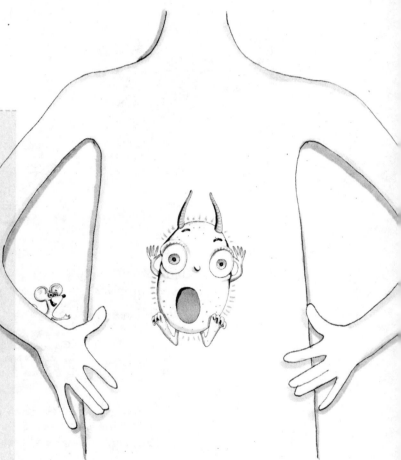

WHAT YOU LEARNED

Making room for worry helps _____

51

Blooming Flower

Here is another way to imagine making more room for your worry. Think about worry as a flower. When you're not worried, the flower is sleeping. When you start to worry, the flower starts blooming and needs more space.

I think of my worry as a sunflower!

COOL FACTS

When we say the name of the emotion in our mind and put a word to how we feel, we can think better and make the emotion feel not so strong.

Write down something that makes you worry.

_____

_____

What kind of flower might your worry be? Draw the flower in this watering can. Give it space to open up its petals. Let your worry, like the flower, just be there. How does it feel?

WHAT YOU LEARNED

I can practice making room for worry by _____

_____

ACTIVITY 21

Your Feelings and You

Have you ever thought of why you have feelings? Especially those no one likes to have, like worry, fear, anger, and sadness? It is because your feelings have a job to do. They are messages from your brain. They are responses to what's happening around you.

Feelings:

- tell you what to pay attention to
- remind you what is important
- help you decide how to act

COOL FACTS

Every child worries sometimes. But did you know that as many as one out of every five kids has a lot of worries that make their life hard?

What do your feelings tell you?

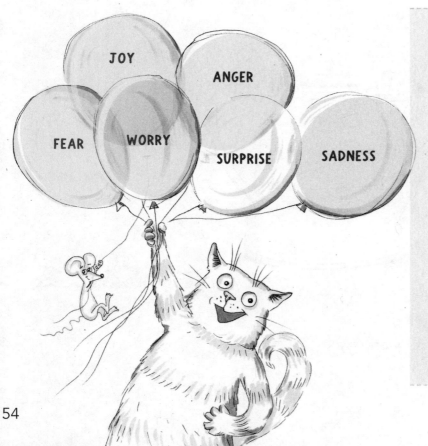

- Notice the six feelings named on the balloons that Curious Cat is holding.
- Read the messages from these feelings on the next page.
- Can you guess what feeling sent each message? Write it on the line that says "from." Start with those that you are surer about.
- Check your answers.

54

Answers: 1. joy; 2. surprise; 3. anger; 4. fear; 5. worry; 6. sadness

What Do Your Feelings Make You Do?

The next time you notice a feeling, try to read what message your brain is sending you. Sometimes it will be an important message, like to duck a ball flying toward you or to be kind to others. At other times, the message might push you to do something that's not helpful, like avoid something important when you worry, or yell, hit, or throw things when you are angry. If this happens, you can let the feeling be and not follow the message.

Read the ideas below. If you think the idea would be good to act on, circle it or put a check mark next to it. If you think the idea is not a useful thing to do, cross it out.

So, the next time you have a big feeling, just think about what it tells you to do and make a good choice. You got this!

What You Learned

Worry communicates that _____

_____

_____

Feelings Finger Puppets

ACTIVITY 22

In this activity, you make your feelings finger puppets by folding paper. You will need six three-inch-square pieces of paper or sticky notes.

1. Fold each square into three equal parts as shown in steps A and B. (If you are using sticky notes, the sticky edge should go on the left side, facing up. Fold the right side first, followed by the left side, so that the sides stick to each other.)

2. Fold about an inch of the top part as shown in step C.

3. Fold the four corners of this folded part backward to create a "face" for each feeling, as shown in step D.

4. Color and decorate your finger puppets. Add happy, worried, angry, or scared faces!

5. Once your finger puppets are ready, come up with a story about your feelings and share it with your family.

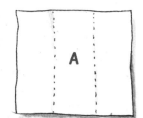
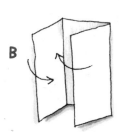

WHAT YOU LEARNED

My feelings are _____ from the brain.

ACTIVITY 23

Make Friends with Your Worry

You learned how to let your worry be, how to make room for it, and how to read messages from your feelings. In this activity, you will practice being friends with your worry. Your mind might be saying: *What? I don't want to be its friend! I hate it!* Can you notice this thought and give it a try anyway? Remember that we talked about how you can feel one way and act a different way? If your mind says, *But why should I?* I'd say because you are learning new skills to deal with worry better. Are you willing to try?

Imagine your worry as a monster. Yes, like one of those from the worry monster family. Do you like any of them more than others? Follow these directions to come up with your own worry monster.

1
Use your imagination to describe your worry monster.

- Is your worry monster big or small?

- What color is your worry monster?

- Does your worry monster have any patterns on its body?

- How many eyes does your worry monster have?

- Does your worry monster have any horns, spikes, or other odd features?

- Does your worry monster have any arms, legs, or wings?

- What kind of sound does your worry monster make?

- How does the worry monster move? Is it slow or fast?

- What does the worry monster eat, if anything?

- Does the worry monster have any friends or family?

- Where does your worry monster live?

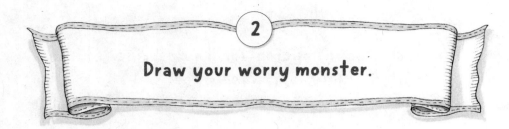

2
Draw your worry monster.

Try to include all the things you imagined when you answered the questions.

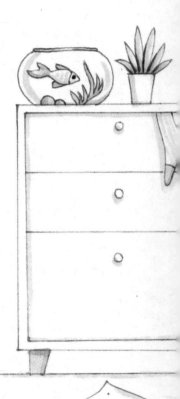

Color and decorate your worry monster. Give it a name.

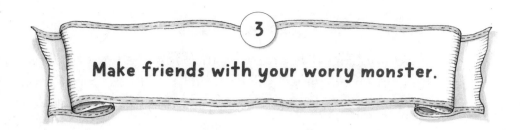

3

Make friends with your worry monster.

For a week, take your worry monster with you wherever you go. Carry it around the house. Put it in your backpack. Bring it on car rides. Take it to playdates. Each time the worry shows up, greet your monster! You can use this book or copy your drawing on a separate paper.

After a week, check to see if your feeling about it changed. I hope you get along a bit better!

WHAT YOU LEARNED

When I become friends with my worry, it _____

_____

_____

Tug-of-War End

When you let your worry be, it is like dropping the rope in a tug-of-war with your worry monster. The worry monster will still be there. But if you stop pulling, the fight ends. If you do that, the worry monster can no longer stop you from doing important things. You can do what you choose to do! And it's okay if your worry monster decides to hang around for a bit.

You have now finished section 3. Congrats! Did you enjoy the Acceptance Ride at the Flex Park? What did you like most in this section?

_____

_____

_____

Come back whenever you want. You know what is coming now, right? Yes, the section quiz and more flex coins to collect.

Section 3 Quiz

1. **When worry shows up, you can**
   a) stop worrying
   b) distract yourself
   c) ask your parent to tell you that there is no need to worry
   d) let your worry be and continue doing what you were doing, the worry won't last forever

2. **You can stop growing worries.**
   a) true
   b) false
   c) not sure
   d) sometimes

3. **When you worry, it is helpful to**
   a) describe what your worry feels like
   b) make room for it
   c) make friends with it
   d) all of the above

4. **Your feelings**
   a) each have a special job to do
   b) are good
   c) are bad
   d) not sure—it is better not to have the bad ones

5. **Accepting feelings means**
   a) naming what you feel
   b) not fighting unpleasant feelings
   c) letting feelings be
   d) all of the above

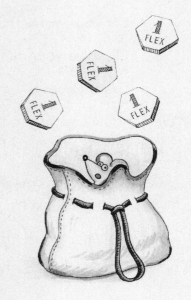

How many flex coins did you get this time? On this page, color the number of coins that you got yellow. Add your total to page 152.

If you missed an answer, look back at the activity that talked about the topic. If you want to take the quiz again, ask a parent to print out a copy.

Answers: 1. d, 2. a, 3. d, 4. a, 5. d

What You Will Learn

In section 4, you will:

- Learn the difference between facts and worry thoughts
- Check out your mind's tricks
- Practice 10 fun ways to make your worry thoughts less powerful
- Let your worry thoughts come and float away
- Observe your mind
- Learn about the quick mind mode

We are now heading to the Unhooking Playground and the Lighthouse of Observation in the Flex Park. Get ready for fun!

 This picture means that the activity has a file you can print.

 This means the activity has an audio file you can listen to.

To get the files, go to *http://www.newharbinger.com/53424*.

Section 4

Unhook from Worry Thoughts

Your mind is the world's most fantastic storyteller. It always comes up with ideas about the world around you. It tells you stories about what is right or wrong, and what you should and should not do. Some of those stories are true. We call those facts. But other stories your mind tells are simply ideas, such as worrying about failing a test or monsters under the bed. You can decide what to do with the story that your mind came up with. You can decide if a story is a fact or simply an idea.

ACTIVITY 24

Facts, Ideas, and Hooks

Let's practice telling the difference between facts and ideas. And let's figure out which ideas tend to hook you. Let me start with a reminder of what a fact is. Guess who will help us?

COOL FACTS

A fact is information that can be checked or proven. It is an actual thing. For example, it's a fact that birds have wings and can fly. Facts help us understand the world around us better. They help us make sense of things.

Fact or Idea?

- Get two different color pens.
- Read the sentences to the right.
- Circle facts in one color.
- Circle ideas in the other color.
- When you finish the activity, check the answers.

1. I will not make any friends at the new school.
2. The earth is round.
3. I will fail the math test.
4. I will not be able to fall asleep tonight.
5. Bees make honey.
6. The moon shines at night.
7. I will get a bad grade on my school project.
8. Tigers' fur has stripes.

Answers: 1, 3, 4, 7 are ideas; 2, 5, 6, 8 are facts.

66

Your Hooks

Even though your ideas are just ideas, they can be very disturbing. They can really hook you. That means you keep worrying about them. Write down some of your hooks in the thought clouds below.

Worry hooks often lead to worry actions.

Your Turn

Draw or write about how worry thoughts hook you and what they can make you do.

_____
_____
_____
_____

WHAT YOU LEARNED

When worry thoughts hook me, I _____

_____

Your Mind's Tricks

ACTIVITY 25

Your mind can play tricks on you. Want to know how? Sure. But first, answer this question. Can you control your thoughts?

_____

Let's see if your answer is correct. To do so, think about ice cream.

Dream of Ice Cream

- What is your favorite flavor of ice cream? _____

  _____

- Cup or cone? _____

- Favorite toppings? _____

  _____

- Is there a special place where you like to get ice cream?

  _____

Draw your favorite ice cream here.

Wow, it looks so yummy!

Now, close your eyes and imagine taking your first bite. Imagine cold, creamy ice cream melting on your tongue.

69

Now, stop thinking about the ice cream. **STOP THINKING.** You can think about anything else: your pet, the book you are reading, your favorite toy, a game. But not the **ICE CREAM**. . .melting on your tongue, with its rich flavor, yummy smell, and delicious toppings. **TRY HARDER!** Circle *yes* if you could stop thinking about ice cream. Circle *no* if you could not.

If you are like me, you circled no.
See what I mean when I say your mind is playing tricks on you?

When you try hard not to think about something, your brain keeps checking if you are still thinking about it. So, the more you try not to think about it, the more you think about it. Tricky, right?

COOL FACTS

Want to learn another trick your brain can play on you? When you worry or have other difficult feelings, you might think that other people around will notice this right away. It seems so because you know about your feelings. But other people actually don't know what is going on inside you.

Bonus Activity

Want to play this trick again? Ask a family member to think of their favorite food, like ice cream or pizza. Tell them to imagine how it looks, tastes, and smells, and then ask them to stop thinking about it. How did they do?

WHAT YOU LEARNED

When I try to control my thoughts, _____

_____

You can't control what comes to your mind, but you can make your worry thoughts lose their power over you. This will help you better control your actions. In the next activities, you will learn how to do that.

Watch Your Mind

ACTIVITY 26

Your mind is always busy thinking. Some of the thoughts it comes up with are important ones, such as remembering to be kind to others. Others are not very important, like daydreaming about flying unicorns. Some, such as your worry thoughts, may not be useful at all. Let's practice watching your mind in action.

1. Set a timer for three minutes.

2. Write down all the thoughts that come to mind or ask your parent to write for you while you name them. If you need more space, use an additional sheet of paper.

3. Look at what you wrote. Underline important thoughts.

4. Did any thoughts surprise or confuse you?

5. Did some thoughts feel like they came from nowhere?

What if I do not have any thoughts? Oh, wait. . . That is a thought, too.

Worry thoughts may seem like they're giving you important messages. But they are actually just thoughts, like any other thoughts. In the next activity, you will practice letting thoughts come and go.

WHAT YOU LEARNED

When I watched my mind, I noticed _____

71

ACTIVITY 27   Leaves on a Stream

This activity will help you practice noticing your thoughts and letting them come and go at their own pace.

Materials: ☐ paper ☐ crayons ☐ scissors ☐ blanket

- First draw leaf shapes on blank paper. Make five or more leaves. See the next page for shape ideas or make up your own. You can also use the leaves from a printed copy of this activity.

- Color in and cut out the leaves.

- Shape a blanket to make a pretend river.

- Sit by the "river" with your leaves ready.

- Start to pay attention to your thoughts.

- When you notice a thought, name it, and put a leaf on the "river."

- Keep doing this with every thought. Move the leaves along the "river" as new thoughts come, making space for new leaves. Practice until you use all your leaves. Then take your leaves out of the "river" and repeat one more time.

When This Activity Can Help You

When you worry, imagine placing your thoughts on leaves and letting them go down a river. There are times when doing this can be helpful, and I came up with some examples for you. Read my ideas and then come up with a couple of your own examples.

- You are in bed and can't fall asleep.
- You have a test tomorrow.
- You have to speak in front of the class.
- You are nervous about going to a new place.
- You feel left out of a group of friends.
- You have a dentist appointment.
- You feel ashamed about a mistake you made.
- You are worried about someone who is sick.

- Your example: _____
- Your example: _____
- Your example: _____

WHAT YOU LEARNED

When I worry, I can practice _____

The next activity will teach fun ways to make your worry thoughts seem less powerful.

THE UNHOOKING TOOLKIT

ACTIVITY 28

Write down some of your worry thoughts:

_____

_____

_____

10 Ways to Take Power Away from Your Worry Thoughts

These 10 ways can help make your worry thoughts seem less powerful. They are tools that you can use when you are hooked by worry. Try them all and then rate each tool on a scale from 10 (your most favorite) to 1 (your least favorite). Add the numbers to the circles and color your three favorite ones!

 Train Cars

Imagine your worry thoughts are like the cars of a fast-moving train. Place thoughts on train cars in your mind and watch the train go by.

 **Character**

Is there a funny movie or a cartoon character you like? Imagine that character saying your thoughts out loud in their voice. Do those thoughts sound a bit silly now?

75

◯ Super Fast

In one word, say what is scariest about your worry. For example, if you're worried about an upcoming test, you can say "fail." Got the word? Now, for 30 seconds, say your worry word as fast as you can and see what happens. Does it still feel as scary? What does it sound like now?

◯ Clouds

Imagine placing your thoughts on clouds and watching them drifting across the sky. Let them come and go at different speeds!

◯ Sing It

Sing your thoughts to the tune of a fun song, like "Happy Birthday" or any other song you like. You can also make up a new song. Do the thoughts now sound more silly than scary?

◯ Super Slow

Say your worry thoughts r-e-a-l-l-y s-l-o-w-l-y as if you are falling asleep or dreaming. Do they seem a bit less scary?

76

◯ A Name and a Voice

You gave your worry monster a name. Now give it a special voice. When worry comes, say, "It is [the name you gave your worry monster] talking." Repeat the thought out loud using your worry monster's voice.

◯ Fun Letters

Write down your worry thoughts using different letters. You can make some letters big and others tiny. You can draw fancy, cursive, or blocky letters. Add cool patterns and designs.

◯ Take It with You

Write down a worry thought on a card or small piece of paper. Tuck the card into a pocket or slip it into your backpack. Carry the card around. See if the words lose power over you after a couple days.

◯ Say It in a Different Language

Do you speak another language? Excellent if you do. If not, that's okay. Ask someone in your family to help you go online. Find out how to say your worry thought in a different language. Write it out and read it out loud. Does worry still show up?

My three favorite tools to take power away from my worry are:

1. _____
2. _____
3. _____

ACTIVITY 29

Become an Observer

In this activity, you will practice rising above your worry thoughts. It is like climbing up to the top of the Observation Tower in the Flex Park. From there, you get the best view. You see all the attractions and can decide where you want to go next.

Gulliver's Adventures

Have you heard of *Gulliver's Travels*? This is a book from a long time ago. Lemuel Gulliver was an adventurous man who went on a journey to explore the world. During his adventures, his ship got caught in a mysterious storm. He was the only one who survived. He ended up on a strange island where only tiny people lived. They thought Gulliver was a giant and called him the "Great Man Mountain." Gulliver enjoyed being big but had to be careful not to step on the little people. After staying on the island for some time, Gulliver left for home. But he got caught in a storm again and did not reach his home. Instead, he ended up in a land of giants. There he was as small as a tiny doll! When he finally returned home, the stories about his adventures became famous in his town and beyond.

When you get hooked by a worry story, you might sometimes feel tiny, like Gulliver did in the Land of Giants, and your worries may appear very big. But when you rise high above your fear, like Gulliver did in the land of tiny people, you can see that worries are not as important as they might seem.

Your Turn

Draw yourself small and your thoughts and feelings very big.

When you are stressed or tired, your brain can become overwhelmed. As a result, you are more likely to believe a thought without stopping to check if it is true or not. When that happens, your brain records the thought as a "truth," and you start to believe it.

Now, draw yourself very big, so that your worry thoughts look very small. Then add 10 things around you. If you draw yourself in your room, add things you have in the room, like your bed, your desk, and toys. If you draw yourself outside, add things you can see outside, like trees, bushes, clouds, birds, and houses.

WHAT YOU LEARNED

When I rise above my worries, _____

_____

Quick Mind Mode

Are you ready to test something else about your mind? I've listed a few words below. When you read each word, write the first thing that pops into your mind. Got it? Let's try.

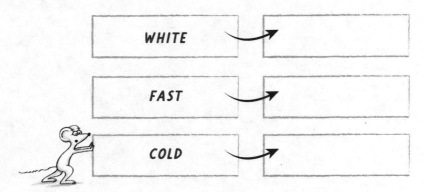

What did you notice about your answers? Is there something in these words that links them? For example, did you come up with the opposite of a word, such as *black* for *white*, *slow* for *fast*, or *hot* for *cold*? Or maybe you wrote something related to the word, like *snow* for *white*, *car* for *fast*, or *ice cream* for *cold*? Write here what you noticed.

_____

_____

Yes, it's interesting to have those answers just pop into your mind, isn't it? I call it **quick mind mode**. *Mode* means a way of doing things a certain way. Sometimes, a quick mind mode is helpful and can make you feel great. For example, when you get lots of ideas, you can come up with a nice drawing.

Or when you play sports, thinking fast helps you be quick in passing a ball or scoring a goal. What are some other times when having a quick mind mode is useful?

_____
_____
_____

But it's very different when your quick mind mode is set to worry. For example, when thoughts about monsters pop up at bedtime. Or when you are studying for a test and your mind keeps coming up with ideas about failing. What are some other times when your quick mind mode is not helpful?

_____
_____
_____

When you get better at noticing your quick mind mode, you can learn to not listen to it when it is not useful. It's like you are the captain of a ship and are steering it in the right direction.

 *Neurons* are cells that work hard every day helping your brain and body send and receive messages through electrical pulses. Did you know that your body has about 86,000,000,000 neurons? That's 86 billion!

WHAT YOU LEARNED

When my thoughts are not helpful, I can _____
_____

ACTIVITY 31 You Are More

You made it to the final activity of the section. You must be very proud of yourself! In this activity you get even better at letting your worry be. You also practice noticing that you are more than your thoughts and feelings.

Imagine yourself as a cookie jar and your thoughts as cookies.

On different cookies, write:

- worries, such as *What if I fail?* or *What if no one likes me?*
- happy thoughts, such as *I love this movie* or *Vacation starts soon*
- everyday thoughts, such as *It's time for lunch* or *I need to make my bed*

If you have real cookies in a cookie jar, you don't grab every single cookie and eat it until the jar is empty, do you? You can do the same thing with your thoughts. You can choose to hold on to some thoughts. Other thoughts are okay to just leave alone. Color only the cookies that you would want to take out of the jar.

On the next page, draw a picture showing that you are much bigger than your thoughts and feelings. Choose one of the ideas below or come up with your own.

- You are the basket. Your thoughts and feelings are the mushrooms.

- You are a poem. Your thoughts and feelings are the words.

- You are a piano. Your thoughts and feelings are keys that play wonderful music with sad and happy notes.

- You are a jewelry box. Your thoughts and feelings are colorful beads.

- You are the sky. Your thoughts and feelings are the stars.

Even though you don't like some of your thoughts and feelings, sometimes they bring a helpful message. It's like a box of colorful markers where every color has a job to do. Color the markers in the box below using different colors for each and write feelings words on them.

WHAT YOU LEARNED

I came up with an idea that my thoughts are like _____,

and I am like _____

Section 4 Quiz

1. **A fact is**
   a) what I think is true
   b) something that can be checked or proven
   c) something I worry about
   d) not sure

2. **Worry thoughts**
   a) can lead to worry actions
   b) are dangerous
   c) can make me think that I must act on them
   d) both a) and c)

3. **I can control my thoughts.**
   a) Always
   b) Sometimes
   c) Never. I tried many times, but they keep coming back!
   d) If I try a bit harder, I can push them away.

4. **I can unhook from worry thoughts by**
   a) practicing the leaves on a stream activity (see page 72)
   b) using the tools from the unhooking toolbox
   c) reminding myself that I am not my thoughts—I am much bigger than these thoughts
   d) all of the above

5. **When I practice leaves on a stream, I**
   a) go outside in the fall and throw leaves in the creek
   b) imagine putting my thoughts on the leaves and letting them come and go
   c) use a special activity when I have worry thoughts
   d) both b) and c) are correct

On this page, color the number of coins that you got yellow. Add your total to page 152.

If you missed an answer, look back at the activity that talked about the topic. If you want to take the quiz again, ask a parent to print out a copy.

Answers: 1. b, 2. d, 3. c, 4. d, 5. d

What You Will Learn

In section 5, you will visit the Flex Park's Mindfulness Valley where you will:

- Practice noticing things that you don't notice when you are hooked by worry
- Learn what mindfulness is and how it can help you cope with worry
- Practice mindful breathing
- Anchor yourself when you feel overwhelmed
- Use your eyes, ears, and nose to come back to the present and unhook from worry
- Practice being curious and attentive
- Play healthy habits bingo

You will also try 10 cool ways to practice mindfulness. Ready? Read on.

 This picture means that the activity has a file you can print.

 This means the activity has an audio file you can listen to.

To get the files, go to *http://www.newharbinger.com/53424*.

Section 5

Mindfulness

Missing Out

Let's check how good you are at noticing things. Worry monsters got scared and hid in this picture. While they worry about something that may never happen, they miss out on 10 wacky things happening here and now.

Grab two pens of different colors. Circle monsters with one color and odd things you spot with another. Check your answers at the end of the book.

What Is Mindfulness?

The Mindfulness Valley in the Flex Park has hills, plains, trees, bushes, lakes, and meadows. Here you practice *mindfulness* and *being mindful*. Wonder what that means? What do you think it means? And how might mindfulness help you? Write your ideas on the lines below.

_____

_____

Thanks for sharing. Read below and circle what you got right.

Being mindful means

- noticing things around you
- noticing things inside you, like your thoughts and feelings
- staying in the present moment
- being flexible in what you focus on
- paying attention fully to what you are doing

Being mindful helps you

- feel calmer and happier more often
- deal with your worries better
- live in the present moment
- focus on important things
- do important things

Being mindful can help you cope with worry. Mindfulness isn't meant to help you relax or calm down. Its goal is to help you notice all that happens here and now. You can then choose to focus on what you think is most important. You can learn to practice it anywhere and anytime!

Paying Attention

I have a challenge for you. Look at the picture below. Pay attention to the things that have fun patterns. Now cover the picture so you can't see it anymore.

Done? Name out loud only the round objects. Uncover the picture and check if you missed any. If you are like me, you missed a few. It is because you told your mind to pay attention to only patterns, not shapes!

It is the same when we are not mindful. We focus on some things and can completely miss others, just like the worry monsters did on the previous page!

WHAT YOU LEARNED

Mindfulness can help me _____

ACTIVITY 33

Being Mindful

When you are not mindful, it is a bit like in the picture on the left. It is as if it is night and the only things you can see are those that moonlight shines on. This is like when you focus only on your worry.

When you are mindful, it is more like in the picture on the right. With the sun shining during the day, you can see many more things. This is like when you know the worry might still be there but you can focus on other things.

Draw yourself when you are not being mindful and notice only your worry. Add thought clouds with your thoughts and feelings.

Draw yourself being mindful. You can draw yourself in your room, at school, or outside. Add thought clouds with your thoughts and feelings. Also draw different things you can spot around you and what you are doing.

WHAT YOU LEARNED

When I am not mindful, _____

_____

ACTIVITY 34 Take a Breath

Breathing is a lovely way to practice being mindful. When you focus on your breath, you slow down and are less overwhelmed by your worry. You also become more aware of what's happening around you. In this activity, you will learn to breathe mindfully. The fun part is that you will do it while caring for thirsty worry monsters. Grab a blue crayon or a marker and read on.

Imagine that each time you breathe out, it's like filling up a jug like this one with water. The jug has lines to show you how much water is in it. When you take a small breath, the water covers only the bottom of the jug. But when you take a very big breath, the water goes up to the top. Ready to practice?

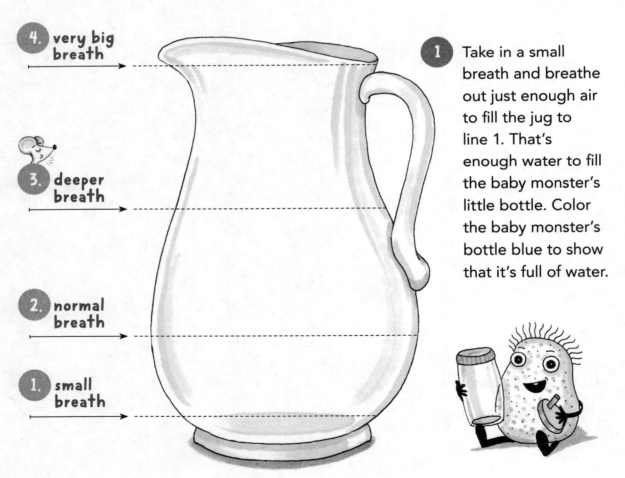

4. very big breath

3. deeper breath

2. normal breath

1. small breath

1. Take in a small breath and breathe out just enough air to fill the jug to line 1. That's enough water to fill the baby monster's little bottle. Color the baby monster's bottle blue to show that it's full of water.

94

2 Take in a normal breath and breathe out enough air to fill the jug to line 2. Is that enough water to fill the water bottles of these three monsters? Color their bottles blue.

3 Take a bigger breath in and breathe out enough air to fill up the jug to line 3. That's enough water for all these thirsty monsters. Color their bottles blue.

4 Take your biggest possible breath in and breathe out air to fill the jug up to line 4—almost to the top. (Take another couple really big breaths, just because it feels good.) Color the giant worry monster's big bottles blue.

Keep Going

The monsters are no longer thirsty. But let's do the activity again. That way, you'll remember it better. Repeat steps 1 to 4. Focus on your breathing.

As you breathe in and out, notice:

- Your shoulders go up and down.
- Your belly pops out and in.
- Your back moves and bends.

1. Start with a small breath in and out.
2. Take a bigger breath in and out.
3. Take an even bigger breath in and out.
4. Take your biggest breath in and out. Repeat, if you'd like.

Great job! What do you notice after practicing mindful breathing? Write on the lines below.

_____

_____

COOL FACTS

When you do mindful breathing, you practice taking deep breaths. Scientists found that deep breathing reduces worry. It also makes you feel calmer and more relaxed. If you practice mindful breathing regularly, you will worry less and deal with worry thoughts better.

WHAT YOU LEARNED

I can practice mindfulness by _____

_____

Anchor Yourself

ACTIVITY 35

Do you know what an *anchor* is? It is the giant heavy metal claw that a ship drops into the water. The anchor grabs the ground tightly when it gets to the bottom of the water. This helps a ship stay in the same place during strong winds or storms.

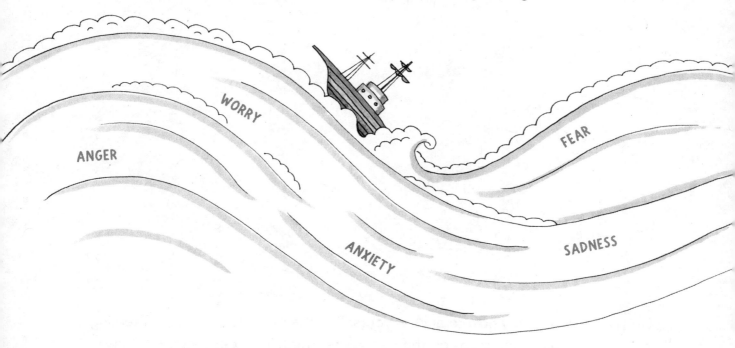

Sometimes, your feelings are like a big storm inside you. You may feel like a boat without an anchor. Strong waves of feelings may seem to toss and turn you around! Color the picture on the next page. Help the ship stay safe through the storm by giving it an anchor that reaches the sea bottom.

Do you want to know how to anchor yourself in the moments when your feelings are strong? Follow the steps on the next page. You might feel better right away after this activity. Or you may still feel worried, and that's fine. When you know how to anchor yourself, you can come back to the present moment faster. This helps you better focus on what is important. It takes only a few minutes. And you can do it anywhere!

Ready, Reset, Go!

1 **Ready? Pay attention.**
(Get the anchor.)

- Find a comfortable place to sit.
- Get ready to pay attention to the present moment.
- Take three slow breaths and notice how your body feels.
- Say hello (or *ahoy*, if you speak Pirate) to your feelings and thoughts.

2 **Reset.** *(Drop the anchor.)*

- Reset your body. Wiggle a bit, stretch, and move from side to side. Move your arms and push your feet into the floor. Pay attention to how your body is moving.

3 **Go!** *(Return back to your life.)*

- Look around.
- Where are you?
- What can you hear?
- What can you notice?
- Go and focus on doing things that are most important to you right now!

99

When do you think this activity will be helpful? List your ideas:

_____
_____
_____

Pirates

Anchors, storms, and sea. I am thinking about pirates. Do you think pirates were afraid of anything? Write your ideas:

_____
_____
_____

PIRATE WORDS
1. *Shiver me timbers.* I'm surprised.
2. *Ahoy.* Hello.
3. *Aye, aye.* I'll get right on that.
4. *Arrr.* I'm happy.

If you answered yes, you are right. Pirates were afraid of storms, believed in myths, and did things that made them feel safer (like you and I sometimes do).

~~Cool Facts~~ STORIES

Do you know why pirates long ago avoided whistling? They thought whistling would cause stormy winds. Pirates also would not let black cats on a ship. They thought black cats brought bad luck!

WHAT YOU LEARNED

When I feel a storm of big feelings, I can anchor myself by taking these three steps:

1. _____
2. _____
3. _____

Look, Listen, and Breathe ACTIVITY 36

In this activity, you will learn how to quickly return to the present moment when you worry, feel another big feeling, or get caught up in your thoughts. Simply follow the three steps below. If you are a bit worried now, it is a perfect time to do it. If not, think of something that happened recently that made you feel worried. Write it here:

_____

_____

_____

Five, Three, One

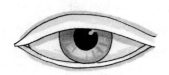

1. **Look around. Notice and name five things you see.** Say the names of the things out loud or in your mind. As you name each one, pause for a few seconds to notice it.

2. **Listen for three sounds.**
    - **A sound far away:** maybe a car roaring, a bird chirping, or a train rumbling
    - **A sound somewhere in your home:** maybe your family talking, a TV playing, or the heater blowing
    - **A sound nearby:** your cat purring, your chair creaking, or a brother or sister playing

3. **Breathe in and notice one smell.** If there is no smell, that's okay. You can smell something, such as a scented pen, a candle, or a drink.

101

How are you feeling now? Did anything change? Write what you notice:

_____

_____

Most of the time, you will feel better after practicing this mindfulness activity. As you start paying attention to things you see, hear, and smell, you focus less on your worry. Can you think of three places where using this activity could be very helpful?

1. _____

2. _____

3. _____

WHAT YOU LEARNED

When I am worried, I can do a quick mindfulness activity, taking these three steps:

1. _____

2. _____

3. _____

THE MINDFULNESS TOOLKIT

ACTIVITY 37

This activity will teach you many different ways to be mindful. You can think of each one as a tool that you can use to practice staying in the present moment. They will also teach you to pay attention to things in a mindful way. When you have tried all 10 tools, rate them from 10 (your most favorite) to 1 (your least favorite). Put the numbers in the circles. Color your top three choices.

10 Ways to Practice Being Mindful

◯ Watch your pet

Look at your pet for two minutes. Name 10 things you noticed. If you don't have a pet, go outside or look out a window. Find a bird or squirrel to watch. Notice the color of its fur or feathers, what it is doing, and the most interesting thing you can spot.

◯ Draw music

Put on your favorite music and grab some paper and markers or crayons. Use shapes, lines, and dots to draw what you hear in the music. Is it happy, sad, or exciting? Can you show how you are feeling in your drawing? Give your art a name and write it down.

103

◯ Notice sounds

Close your eyes and listen. How many sounds can you hear? Listen for the ones farthest away. Then listen for sounds that are closer. Try this activity with a parent, brother, sister, or friend. See who can notice more sounds!

◯ Breathe and slide beads

Thread five beads on a pipe cleaner and twist both ends, keeping the beads close to one end. Take five deep breaths. Each time you exhale, move one bead to the other end of the pipe cleaner. Pay attention to how each bead feels and how it moves.

◯ Brush teeth

Use your senses when brushing your teeth. Can you feel the toothpaste foam in your mouth? What does it taste like? How does it smell? Is the water you rinse with warm or cold? How many things can you notice about brushing your teeth?

◯ Make nature art

Gather 10 nature objects, like rocks, leaves, sticks, pine cones, or flower petals. Arrange them to make an art piece. Pay attention to patterns, shapes, and colors. Take a photo of your art and share it with your friends and family!

◯ Eat mindfully

Grab a cookie or a piece of dry fruit. Look at it, paying attention to every detail—its color, shape, smell, and texture. Slowly take a tiny bite. Is it crunchy, chewy, or gooey? What does it taste like? Name everything you notice about its flavor. Eat it slowly, enjoying every bit.

◯ Draw with your eyes closed

Grab a piece of paper and a marker or crayon. Choose a simple object, like a cup, a pen, or a flowerpot. Look at its shape attentively and try to remember it. Now, try to draw it with your eyes closed. How did it turn out?

◯ Explore a toy

Hold your favorite toy, such as a stuffed animal. Spend a few minutes describing every detail you see. How does it feel in your hands? Is it soft, squishy, or bumpy? What makes it special to you?

◯ Drink through a straw

Grab a straw and a glass of your favorite drink. Slowly sip your drink through the straw. Taste its sweetness, sourness, or freshness, savoring every sip!

My three favorite mindfulness tools from this activity are:

1. _____
2. _____
3. _____

ACTIVITY 38 Make a Healthy Habits Checklist

In this activity, you will learn about healthy habits and play a special game of bingo with your family. A *habit* is something you do regularly. A *healthy habit* is an activity that helps your body and mind stay strong and healthy. When you are strong and healthy, you deal with worry better. Healthy habits also help you feel happier more often.

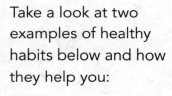

Take a look at two examples of healthy habits below and how they help you:

- **Habit:** brushing your teeth every morning and night
- **Benefits:** keeps your teeth clean and helps you avoid cavities

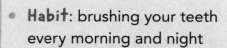
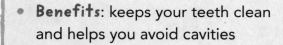

- **Habit:** eating fruits and vegetables every day
- **Benefits:** gives your body vitamins and energy

COOL FACTS

Your brain needs a lot of energy to work. It needs almost the same energy when you are awake and when you are asleep, when you rest and when you are active. It is because it is taking care of you all the time!

106

Healthy Habits

- Grab two markers of different colors.
- Use one marker to circle the activities below that you already do. They are helping you take good care of your mind and body.
- Then use a different color marker to circle the activities you don't do yet but want to do.

1. Eat fruits and vegetables every day
2. Drink plenty of water every day
3. Brush teeth in the morning and before bed
4. Get 9 to 12 hours of sleep every night
5. Play every day
6. Exercise and stay active one hour or more per day
7. Limit screen time to one to two hours a day
8. Learn something new every day
9. Be kind and say thank you to others for their help
10. Take good care of things and keep them in their place
11. Spend time outside every day
12. Eat healthy snacks, such as fruits
13. Share your feelings with parents or other adults you trust
14. Spend time with family
15. Take care of your pet

16. Help with chores
17. Do a creative activity (like art or a craft) every day

Healthy Habits Bingo

Look at the tasks listed on this bingo card. Do as many of these tasks from this bingo card as you can every day during the next week. Color the squares where you did the task. To win, color five squares in a line going up and down, from side to side, or from one corner to another corner.

HEALTHY HABITS BINGO

Name: _____

Ate a healthy snack	Said thank you three times	Cleaned my room	Had five or more cups of water	Learned a new thing
Did a chore	Spent an hour outside	Played sports	Ate one vegetable	Made my bed
Played a game with my family	Looked after my pet	FREE	Ate two fruits	Took a shower or bath
Did a craft or art	Helped family or a friend	Shared my feelings	Went to bed on time	Played with a friend
Brushed my teeth in the morning and evening	Packed my lunch myself	Packed and unpacked my backpack	Named five things I am thankful for	Read a book

WHAT YOU LEARNED

I want to work on these healthy habits: _____

_____

Section 5 Quiz

1. **When I am mindful, I**
   a) notice more things here and now
   b) can choose what to focus on
   c) notice my thoughts and feelings
   d) all of the above

2. **To practice mindfulness, I can**
   a) focus on my breathing
   b) anchor myself
   c) name five things I see, three sounds I hear, and one thing I smell
   d) all of the above

3. **Practicing mindfulness means**
   a) pushing worry thoughts away
   b) staying in the present moment
   c) relaxing
   d) all of the above

4. **A healthy habit is**
   a) an activity that helps you be healthier and happier
   b) something you do regularly
   c) a habit you need to get rid of
   d) both a) and b) are correct

5. **Pick a healthy habit**
   a) hiding your feelings (no one should know about them!)
   b) watching TV for at least three hours daily (it is so fun!)
   c) spending time outside every day
   d) playing on your phone in bed

On this page, color the number of coins that you got yellow. Add your total to page 152.

If you missed an answer, look back at the activity that talked about the topic. If you want to take the quiz again, ask a parent to print out a copy.

Answers: 1. d, 2. d, 3. b, 4. d, 5. c

What You Will Learn

You've come a long way in the book! In section 6, you will:

- Think about your strengths and qualities you admire in others
- Learn about values
- Create your own superhero badge
- Write about what is important to you and what makes you happy
- Learn how knowing what is important can help you make better decisions
- Work on making your life more fun and exciting
- Take brave actions

Are you ready? Let's keep exploring the Flex Park and visit the Island of Values!

 This picture means that the activity has a file you can print. To get the files, go to *http://www.newharbinger.com/53424*.

Your Heart's Secrets

From Mindfulness Valley in the Flex Park, you walk over a small bridge to get to the Island of Values. There, you find a giant treasure chest. That's exciting! But wait. It is not filled with gold or jewels. Are you a bit disappointed? Don't be. Inside that chest, you find something very special to you. Something that can't be bought with money. Only you know what you want it to be and dream it will be. Inside the chest above, draw or write about your treasure.

ACTIVITY 39

Your Strengths

We haven't yet talked much about your strengths. Is it okay to ask you to share them? If thoughts like *I don't know what my strengths are* or *I'm not good at anything* show up, that's okay. Many people have those thoughts. This activity will help you look at what you are good at and share anyway, even if your mind gives you those thoughts.

Things You Love

Read the questions below. Use your answers to create a story about things you like. Draw or write your story in the film frames.

- What is your best memory?
- What do you wish your family and friends knew about you?
- What is your favorite movie or book?
- What is your favorite food?
- What do you like about yourself?
- What makes you happy?
- Who inspires you?
- What inspires you?

Asking Questions

Curious Cat wants to ask some people you know questions about you. Who do you want Curious Cat to talk to?

- Draw those people's pictures and write their names.
- Put your name in the blank space in Curious Cat's questions.
- What do you think those people would answer?

To a teacher:
What is _____ best at?

To a friend:
What does _____ like to do for fun?

COOL FACTS

Did you know that smells can make you recall memories tied to strong feelings? For example, when you smell a freshly baked pizza, you might think of your best friend's birthday party and remember that you felt happy there.

To a coach:
What helps _____ get better?

To family:
What is special about _____ ?

I hope that Curious Cat's questions helped you think better about what your strengths might be. If not, no worries. The next activities will help you understand more about them.

WHAT YOU LEARNED

My strengths include: _____

ACTIVITY 40 Things That Matter

Think of someone who is important to you. It can be someone you know and admire, like a teacher, relative, or friend. Or it can be your favorite hero. Write their name here:

_____

What do you like most about this person?
Here are some ideas of what you might like:

- how they treat other people
- how they solve problems
- how they always have fun
- how kind they are
- how brave they are

List things that inspire you about your hero here:

_____

_____

_____

Read what you wrote and pick the three things that are most important to you. Are they things that you also want to be able to do? Are these qualities you want to have? If so, they are your *values*. Your values are things that are really important to you. They also tell how you want to treat other people. Knowing your values helps you make good choices. And acting on your values makes life more joyful and gives it more meaning!

COOL FACTS

Did you know that a brain reaches its largest size when a person is 11 to 14 years old?

Light 'em Up!

Look at these pictures of light bulbs. Each has a word to describe a quality of a person. Choose three to five bulbs with qualities that are the most important to you. Color them yellow to light them up.

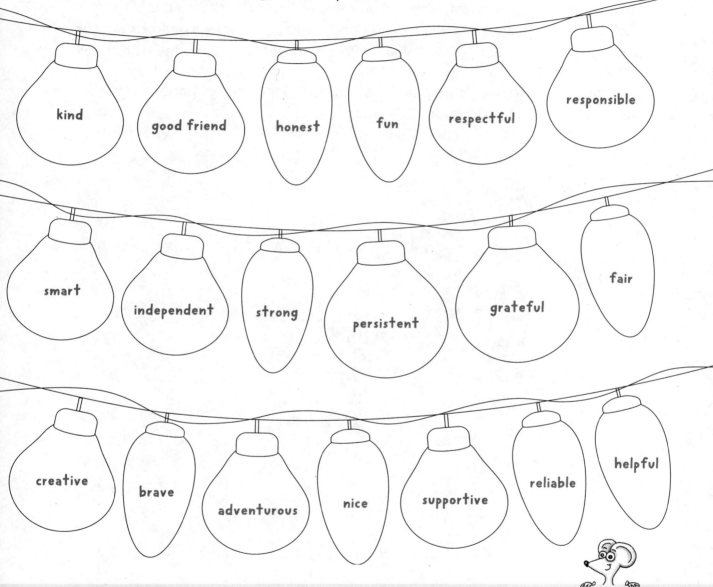

WHAT YOU LEARNED

Knowing my values is important because _____

ACTIVITY 41 Your Superhero Badge

In this activity, you will make your own superhero badge to show three to five values you chose in the last activity. You can use a word or draw a picture for each value. For example, if you picked "kind," you could draw a heart or write the word kind. If you chose "brave," you could draw a sword or write the word brave.

Choose one of the badge shapes below. Copy it on a piece of paper. Add your value words or pictures. Color it the way you'd like!

Carry your badge with you. You can place it on the cover of a notebook, hang it up on your bedroom door, or frame it and put it on your wall. You can also add the badge to your superhero costume that you drew on page 22.

As you grow older, your values may change. This happens because you learn new things, and your interests change. You can add values that become important to you to your badge or make a new one.

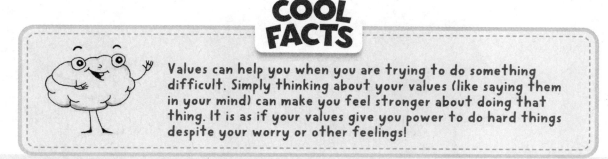

COOL FACTS

Values can help you when you are trying to do something difficult. Simply thinking about your values (like saying them in your mind) can make you feel stronger about doing that thing. It is as if your values give you power to do hard things despite your worry or other feelings!

WHAT YOU LEARNED

My most important values that I put on my badge are _____

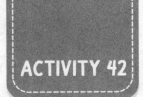

ACTIVITY 42 What Makes You Happy?

In this activity, let's put together things that bring you joy and happiness.

1 In the circles on the clock, write names of family members, friends, and pets who are important to you. Also include activities that make you happy.

2 On a piece of colored paper, draw a clock hand. You can copy the shape of the clock hand on the next page, if you'd like, or draw a clock hand yourself. Cut it out.

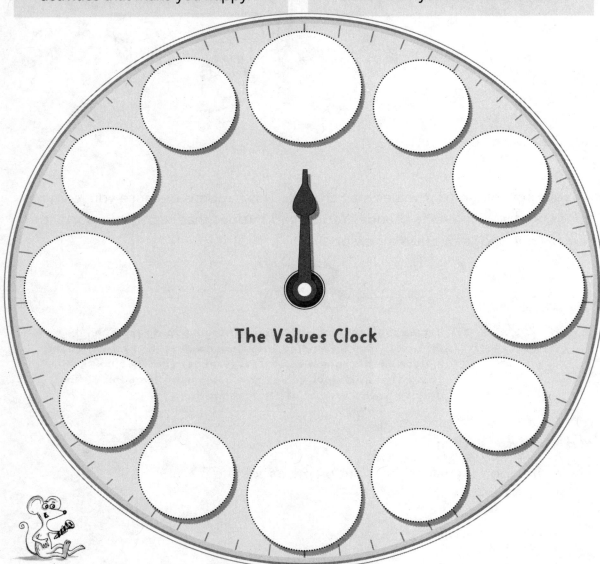

The Values Clock

120

3 Point the hand to different circles on the clock. Pause on each, and for a moment, think of how you feel when you are with this person or when you do this activity.

4 In the big heart below, write pleasant feelings and thoughts that came to mind when you moved the clock hand around. Use different color markers or crayons.

WHAT YOU LEARNED

I feel happy when I am with _____

and when I do _____

121

ACTIVITY 43

Fun with What Matters

In this activity, you will focus on the actions you can take to bring more fun into your life. Sometimes, when you're worried, you stop paying attention to the things that make you happy. In the last activity, you put things that you value on a clock. When you stop paying attention to those things, it's like your values clock stops. But at any moment, you can choose to turn the clock back on by doing things you love and spending time with people who are important to you!

COOL FACTS

When you do something that's hard for you to do, like listening to classical music or reading a more advanced book, it makes you learn and get smarter. But did you know you also boost your imagination and become more creative?

Time for Fun

1. Choose four important things you put on your clock in the previous activity. In the four circles on the next page, write those four things.

2. Under each of those circles, write how you can enjoy doing that thing or being with that person.

Examples:
Family: play a board game, go out for ice cream, read a book, or stargaze
Art: visit an art gallery, create a collage, decorate a rock, or learn to knit

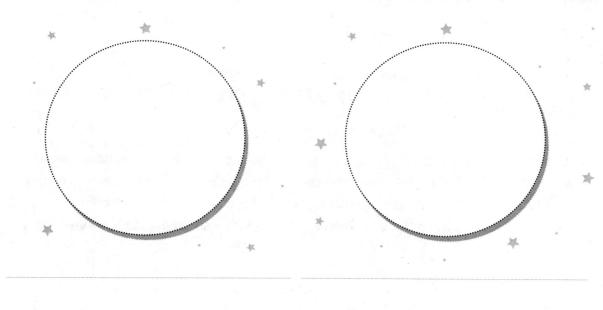

WHAT YOU LEARNED

I can _____ (activity)

with _____ (name).

This can make me feel _____ .

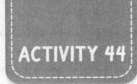

ACTIVITY 44

Brave You

In this activity, you will think about acting bravely. But first you look at how Curious Cat acts bravely. See the tall mountain on the next page? Curious Cat wants to get to the top. He thinks that from up there, he can get the best view of the Flex Park. He also wants to enjoy the night sky when it gets dark. Guess what? He is very worried.

The mountain is too tall! I am scared of spiders, getting lost, storms, strong winds, steep slopes, and falling!

Curious Cat decides to make room for his worries and sets out on his journey. He takes the Toward Road. As he climbs up, he practices being present and noticing what's happening around him. He thinks of his values, like being adventurous, curious, creative, and a good friend. That helps him keep going despite his worries. When he makes it to the top, he is very proud of himself. His worries are still there. But the view is worth it!

Your Turn

Ready to practice being brave? Okay, imagine you have a mountain to climb.

1 What is at the top that you want to get to or do?
What is your action goal? Write it here:

_____

_____

2 Draw a curvy, long road to the top. When you want something in life, your path is often not smooth. You usually need to put in some hard work!

3 Add some fun things you can stop and do on your way. Look at the things on your values clock or in activity 43 for ideas.

4 Do you want someone to come with you? Write their name on the line below or draw them if you'd like.

_____

5 How will you feel when you get to the top?

_____

_____

_____

COOL FACTS

Did you know that when you learn something that you are really interested in, your brain will remember that thing better?

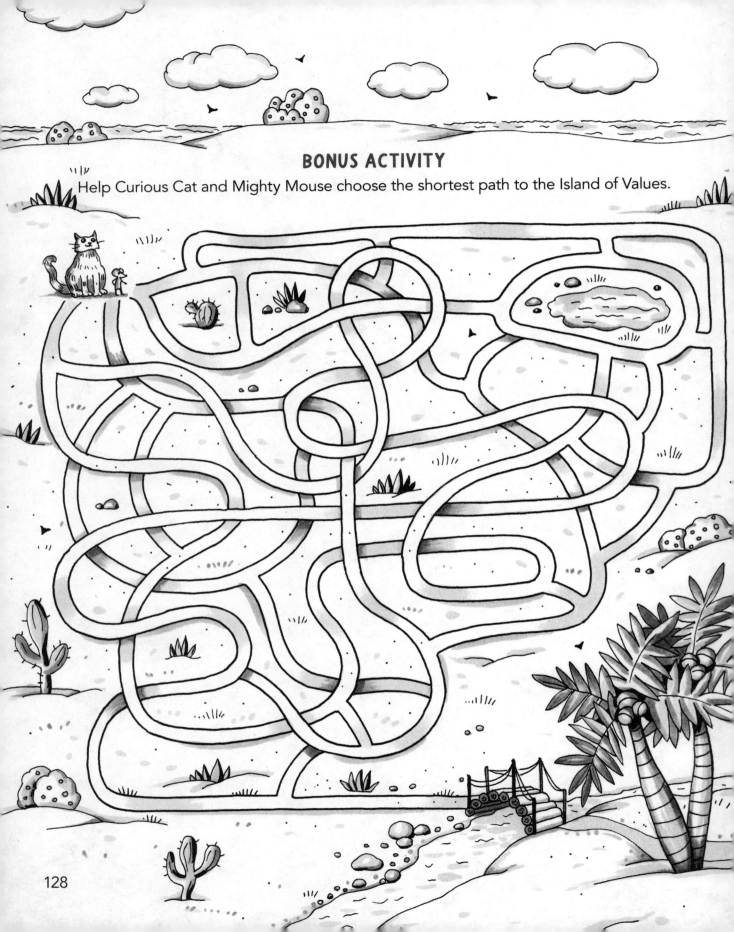

BONUS ACTIVITY
Help Curious Cat and Mighty Mouse choose the shortest path to the Island of Values.

Section 6 Quiz

1. I can make better decisions
   a) when I know my values
   b) when I am angry
   c) when I am worried
   d) when I act fast

2. I can be happier when I
   a) spend time with somebody I love
   b) push worries away
   c) do things that are important
   d) both a) and c) are correct

3. Taking the Toward Road means
   a) moving toward my goals
   b) knowing my values
   c) doing things that are important to me, even when I worry
   d) all of the above

4. An example of a value is
   a) kind
   b) brave
   c) money
   d) a) and b) are correct

5. My superhero badge
   a) tells everyone that I am a superhero
   b) reminds me of what is important and how I want to be
   c) means I am special
   d) is part of my Halloween costume

On this page, color the number of coins that you got yellow. Add your total to page 152.

If you missed an answer, look back at the activity that talked about the topic. If you want to take the quiz again, ask a parent to print out a copy.

Answers: 1. a, 2. d, 3. d, 4. d, 5. b

What You Will Learn

In section 7, you will check out the Commitment Corner of the Flex Park to:

- Set a SMART goal
- Learn about obstacles, which are things that get in your way when you move toward your goals
- Come up with a plan for overcoming your worry
- Discover why being kind to yourself is important
- Practice being kind to yourself
- Play a special kind of tic-tac-toe
- Check to see if your mind has become more flexible

You will also count all the flex coins you've earned on page 152. After that, you will get a special award for all the hard work you did in this book!

 This picture means that the activity has a file you can print. To get the files, go to *http://www.newharbinger.com/53424*.

Section 7
You Can Do It

The Story of the Frog That Kept Trying

Once upon a time, two frogs fell into a jar of cream. They wanted to escape but couldn't. They could not jump out, because the jar was deep. And their legs did not reach the bottom.

One of the frogs got tired fast and gave up. The other frog kept pushing and kicking, and pushing and kicking. It refused to give up!

After hours of work, something surprising happened. The cream changed. The frog has beaten it up into solid butter. When that happened, the frog could jump out of the jar!

Why do you think I told you this story? Write your ideas below. Then, keep reading.

ACTIVITY 45 Set a SMART Goal

You're in the Commitment Corner of the Flex Park. Here you start doing things you want. You don't let your worry stop you. You keep trying, and you act bravely! Can you think of something daring you want to do this week? Great. In this activity, you will learn to set what's called a **SMART goal**.

S stands for **specific**.
Decide what exactly you want to do. For example, instead of saying, *I will talk to my friends more*, you can plan, *I will speak to one friend every day*.

M stands for **meaningful**.
Your goal has to be about something *important* to you, something you want. Why is this goal important to you?

A stands for **adds to your life**.
How will reaching this goal make your life better?

R stands for **realistic**.
Being *realistic* means that it can actually happen in real life. Your goal is about something you can do. For example, imagine you want to read a book. It could be too long to read the whole book in a day. So, it may not be realistic. Instead, you may decide to read a page or a chapter each day.

T stands for **timed**.
Timed means that you will plan how long it will take to reach the goal. You will also set a specific time to do it. For example, *I will finish my painting by the end of the week* or *I will practice piano for 15 minutes every day in the evening*.

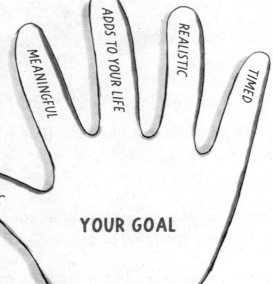

YOUR GOAL

COOL FACTS

Did you know that if you tell your friend or your family member about the goal you set, it will help you move toward it? This happens because it is important to be true to your word!

132

Look at Curious Cat's example below. Then set one SMART goal for yourself.

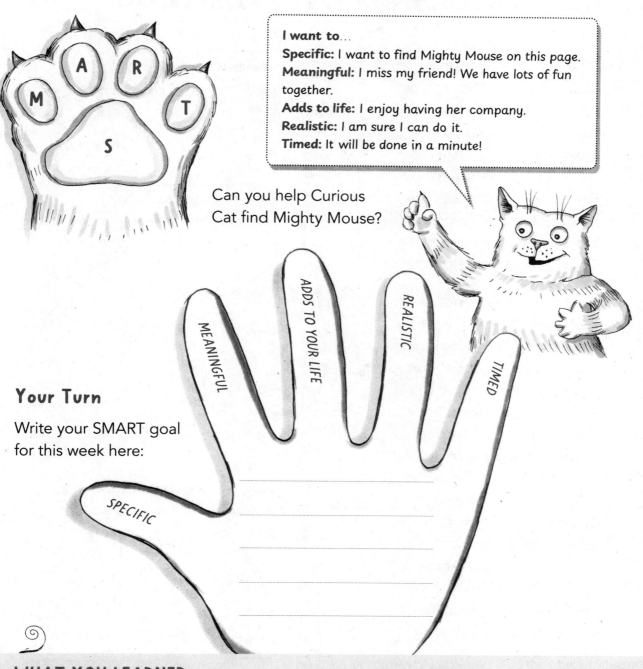

I want to...
Specific: I want to find Mighty Mouse on this page.
Meaningful: I miss my friend! We have lots of fun together.
Adds to life: I enjoy having her company.
Realistic: I am sure I can do it.
Timed: It will be done in a minute!

Can you help Curious Cat find Mighty Mouse?

Your Turn

Write your SMART goal for this week here:

WHAT YOU LEARNED

SMART stands for a goal that is _____

ACTIVITY 46

Jump Over Obstacles

Obstacles are things that get in your way. They can be physical things, like obstacle courses on a sports day. Most kids find obstacle courses fun. They like to jump over the hurdles, climb up the walls, and go on their bellies under the low bars! Do you like obstacle courses?

Obstacles can also be problems that get in your way. Thoughts and feelings can become your obstacles. For example, when difficult thoughts and feelings hook you, it can make it harder to meet your goals or do important things. It can also become an obstacle when you don't know how to do something, or you don't have the help you need. At the Commitment Corner of the Flex Park, you learn to deal with such obstacles.

Let's practice identifying obstacles while helping Curious Cat and Mighty Mouse.

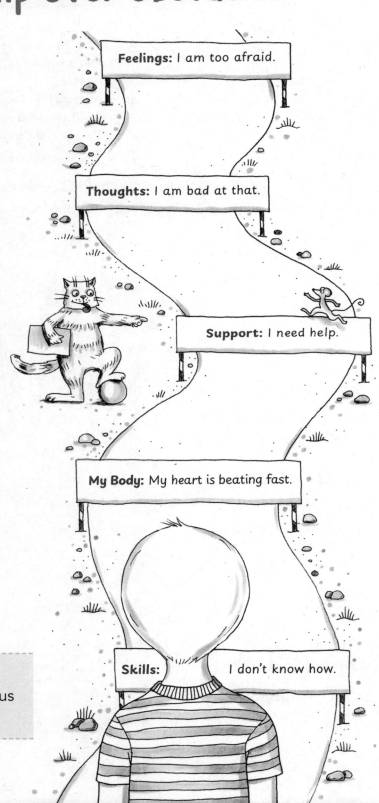

Feelings: I am too afraid.

Thoughts: I am bad at that.

Support: I need help.

My Body: My heart is beating fast.

Skills: I don't know how.

Curious Cat climbed a really tall tree and is afraid to get down. Mighty Mouse wants to help him get down.

- Help Mighty Mouse find the shortest path to Curious Cat. Draw a line that goes around obstacles.
- Can you think of some other obstacles Curious Cat and Mighty Mouse might need to deal with?
- Can you help them deal with obstacles caused by big feelings using ideas you learned in this book?
- Are there items that could help them? I drew some options. Draw anything else you think that Mighty Mouse can use to help Curious Cat get down.

135

Your Turn

Think about the SMART goal you set in the previous activity. What are some obstacles that you might have to deal with when you work on it? Write your answers.

Difficult feelings:

_____

Difficult thoughts:

_____

Skills I need:

_____

Help I need:

_____

Other obstacles:

_____

_____

How can you deal with those obstacles? Write about some skills you learned in this book that could help you.

_____

_____

_____

WHAT YOU LEARNED

When I start doing hard things, I may have to deal with _____

Your Plan for Dealing with Worry

ACTIVITY 47

You won't believe it. You are just three activities away from the end of the book! My friends and I already miss you! It is a good time to come up with a plan for dealing with your difficult feelings and thoughts when you finish the book. In this activity, you will create your plan for dealing with your worry.

Make It Fun

Choose one of the ideas below to make your plan for dealing with worry. Or come up with your own idea for your plan.

> Make your plan in the form of a tree. Use roots for your values, a trunk for your goals, branches for your favorite tools, and clouds for obstacles.

> Draw your plan as a map of an island. Use buried treasures for your goals. Fill the road to the treasures with obstacles. Add your values as special places on the island.

> Create your own amusement park where different places have different tools from this book that can help you deal with worry.

> Draw your plan as an obstacle course. The prize at the end is your goal.

Turn the page to start working on your plan.

My Plan for Dealing with Worry

To create your plan:

- Pick three goals for dealing with worry.
- List three of your most important values.
- Add obstacles you might face.
- Add tools that you learned from this book to deal with obstacles.

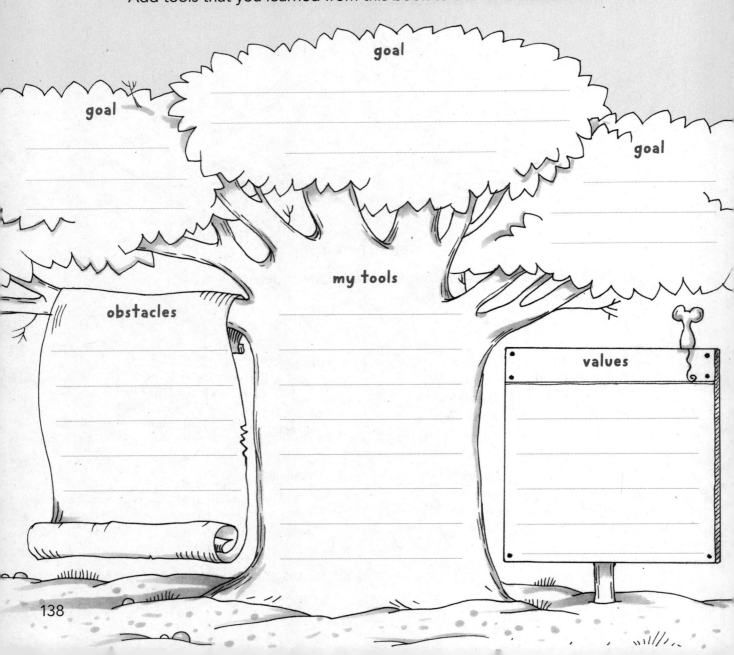

# My Plan for Dealing with Worry

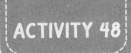

ACTIVITY 48

Be Kind to Yourself

Can you think about a moment when a friend or family member was sad? Maybe it was because they made a mistake, something difficult happened, or their feelings got hurt.

Did you say nice words or give them a hug? If you did, this means you tried to understand their feelings and be kind to them. I am sure that this helped them feel better. When you treat others with kindness, it feels good to them, and it feels good to you!

When you worry, you can treat yourself kindly. It is like being a good friend to yourself when things are not great. Wonder how to do that? You may say encouraging words to yourself. You can remind yourself that you are strong. You can remind yourself that others feel the same way sometimes.

When you treat yourself kindly, it is like giving a flower sunlight and water. Draw yourself as a flower. Add sunlight and water.

Me as a flower

Kindness Reminder

This sign teaches you steps to treat yourself kindly. You can use it as a reminder to be kind to yourself when you worry, feel bad about a mistake, or are upset. You can also use it when you have other difficult feelings.

Color the inside of the triangle yellow.

In the top circle, draw an eye. This is to remind you to pause and notice your difficult feelings and thoughts.

In the lower left circle, draw a heart and color it red. This is to remind you to do something kind for yourself. You can do something you enjoy or say nice words to yourself. For example, you can say, Worry will pass or It's hard, but I can do it or I can be kind to myself.

In the lower right circle, add two faces to the one I drew there. This is to remind you that you are not alone when you worry. Many kids and adults often feel the same way.

COOL FACTS

 Did you know that when you practice being kind to yourself, your mind becomes more flexible? You also don't compare yourself to others as much, worry less, and let go of mistakes more easily! Isn't that cool?

Write some ideas of how to be kind to yourself.

_____
_____
_____
_____
_____

WHAT YOU LEARNED

When I am kind to myself, it helps _____

_____

Being Kind Tic-Tac-Toe

ACTIVITY 49

In this activity, you will learn to be kind to yourself by playing a special tic-tac-toe game with a parent or sibling. You can copy the game card on the next page. You can also put a copy on the fridge to see and use.

1. Write your name and the name of the other player at the top of the chart.

2. Each player picks a crayon or marker in a different color.

3. When a player feels worried or sad, they choose an activity from the game card. Then they color in the box with that activity.

4. Whoever fills in three boxes in a row first wins. The three boxes can go up and down, side to side, or from one corner to another corner.

BEING KIND TIC-TAC-TOE
Things you can do when you worry or feel sad

Player 1 Name: _____ Color: _____
Player 2 Name: _____ Color: _____

Say to yourself, I am sorry you feel that way.	Name the feeling and allow yourself to feel it.	Tell yourself it is okay to make mistakes.
Write a thank-you note to yourself for something nice you did today.	Draw a heart. Inside write things that make you special.	Ask: What would you tell a friend if they worried about that same thing?
Do something you enjoy doing.	Remind yourself that all people feel this way sometimes.	Say I love you to yourself.

WHAT YOU LEARNED

When I worry, I can be kind and do these things: _____

_____

How Flexible Are You Now?

ACTIVITY 50

Wow! It's been a long journey. You have arrived at the very end of the book. Congrats on all the hard work! Do you remember that you answered questions at the start of the book to see how flexible your mind was? In this activity, you will do it again to see if anything has changed.

How Flexible Is Your Mind Now?

1. Read each sentence below.

2. Circle the number of points that show how true the idea is for you.

3. Add up the points. You earn one flex coin for each point. Add your total to page 152.

	Not at all true	Pretty true	True	Very true
Worry makes my life hard.	3	2	1	0
I wish I had a magic wand to make my worries disappear.	3	2	1	0
To have a good life, I need to get rid of my worries and fears.	3	2	1	0
If I worry, that means the bad thing will happen.	3	2	1	0
I always try to get rid of bad thoughts and feelings.	3	2	1	0
Worrying is terrible. I can't stand it.	3	2	1	0
I am afraid of trying new things.	3	2	1	0
When I worry, I don't do things that are important to me.	3	2	1	0

When I worry, I do worse at school.	3	2	1	0
If I worry, something must be wrong with me.	3	2	1	0
Until worry goes away, I can't make friends.	3	2	1	0
Until fear goes away, I can't try new things.	3	2	1	0
I worry a lot about what others think about me.	3	2	1	0
Total points				

Total points

WHAT YOU LEARNED

Look back at activity 5 on page 11 to see how many points you earned the first time you answered these questions. Compare it to your total points this time.

The total number of points is (circle one):

higher

lower

the same

My mind is (circle one):

more flexible

less flexible

the same as before

Write what you noticed:

146

Section 7 Quiz

1. **A SMART goal means**
   a) something I can do
   b) something important to me
   c) something that improves my life
   d) all of the above

2. **Dealing with obstacles when you have a goal means**
   a) not paying attention to worry
   b) jumping high
   c) using tools that help you move toward your goal
   d) running away from worry

3. **My plan for dealing with worry includes**
   a) things that are important to me—my values
   b) helpful tools I can use that I learned in this book
   c) goals I want to reach
   d) all of the above

4. **Being kind to myself is**
   a) not necessary—I can manage without being kind to myself
   b) helpful in dealing with worry and other difficult feelings
   c) helpful in developing a flexible mindset
   d) both b) and c) are correct

5. **I can practice being kind to myself by**
   a) telling myself it is okay to worry sometimes
   b) thinking of what I would tell a friend if they were worried
   c) doing something I like
   d) all of the above

On this page, color the number of coins that you got yellow. Add your total to page 152.

If you missed an answer, look back at the activity that talked about the topic. If you want to take the quiz again, ask a parent to print out a copy.

Answers: 1. d, 2. c, 3. d, 4. d, 5. d

Time to Say Goodbye

My dear friend, it is time for us to say goodbye to each other. I hope you enjoyed this book and will keep it on your bookshelf. Maybe you will pull it out from time to time to review your tools or to say hi to Curious Cat, Might Mouse, and the worry monsters! They will miss you and be happy to see you again. I will, too. I want to thank you for making it to the very end. I can't wait to hear what you think about this book. Did it help you deal with your worries? You can send an email to me at *kidswhoworryworkbook@gmail.com*.

It's time to look at your total number of flex coins on page 152. Got the number? Now look at the awards on the next three pages. Which one matches your number of flex coins? Write down your total number of coins and add your name to your award!

Now hop on the Flex Wheel in the Flex Park to celebrate your hard work and your award!

Awards

Number of flex coins (from 30 to 40): _____

A Flexible Mindset

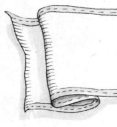 # ACHIEVER

Is Presented To

Name: _____

For having fun while practicing all the activities in
A Workbook for Kids Who Worry
and for great work on developing a flexible mindset

Date: _____

Book Author: *Anna Scetinina*

Number of flex coins (from 41 to 60): _____

A Flexible Mindset

CHAMPION

Is Presented To

Name: _____

For having fun while practicing all the activities in

A Workbook for Kids Who Worry

and for developing a flexible mindset
and using ACT skills

Date: _____

Book Author: *Anna Scetinina*

Number of flex coins (61 or more): _____

A Flexible Mindset

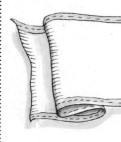

MASTER

Is Presented To

Name: _____

For having fun while practicing all the activities in
A Workbook for Kids Who Worry,
for developing a flexible mindset
and becoming excellent at using ACT skills
and tools from this book

Date: _____

Book Author: *Anna Scetinina*

Count Your Flex Coins

In this chart, write the total number of flex coins you earned next to each quiz or activity listed.

Activity 5: Do You Have a Flexible Mindset?	
Section 1 Quiz	
Section 2 Quiz	
Section 3 Quiz	
Section 4 Quiz	
Section 5 Quiz	
Section 6 Quiz	
Section 7 Quiz	
Activity 50: How Flexible Are You Now?	
Total flex coins:	

Check Your Answers

Visual answer to activity 8, word search

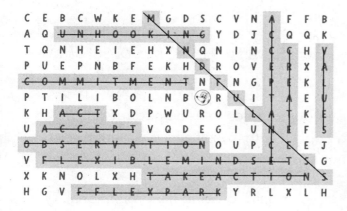

Visual answer to Intro to Section 5

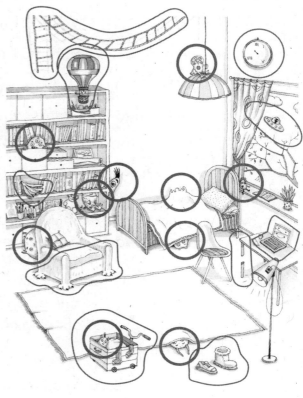

Visual answer to activity 17, nesting dolls

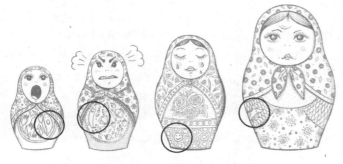

Visual answer to activity 44, maze

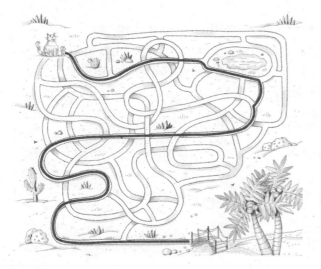

Visual answer to activity 46, maze

153

Acknowledgments

Many people have encouraged, supported, and guided me in writing and illustrating this workbook, and I wish to thank all of them.

First and foremost, thank you to ACT founders Steven C. Hayes, Kirk D. Strosahl, and Kelly G. Wilson.

A special thank you to Russ Harris, whose books and courses helped me fall in love with ACT and learn how to use and apply it with myself and my clients. I also want to thank Russ for his encouragement and support.

Thank you to Anna Prudovski for taking me on board, guiding my professional growth, supporting me in difficult moments, appreciating my creativity, and offering thoughtful advice and feedback as I created this book.

Thank you to Victoria Prooday. Without her support, I would not have dared to change my career and become a psychotherapist. She helped me connect my artistic side and my values of being helpful and caring, and taught me to look for a miracle in every child.

Thank you to my professor Thomasina Odom Lawson. When she said, "I can't wait to see your book published," I had no idea that this dream of mine would ever come true. (Even as I am writing this, it still seems unreal.)

I want to gratefully acknowledge the wonderful team at New Harbinger Publications. Thank you for reaching out to me, trusting me in the process, and providing so much guidance and support. I especially want to thank Wendy Millstine, Madison Davis, Elizabeth Dougherty, and Amy Shoup for all the help they have given me throughout the publishing process.

Thank you to my caring friend Anne Marie for all her incredible support and insightfulness.

I want to thank my husband, Alex, and my son, Elliott, for their continuous excitement about my book, for helping my dream come true, and for providing me with suggestions, support, and care throughout the journey. Thank you to my grandma for raising me to be who I am and finding value in anything I created. Thank you to my parents for supporting my artistic endeavours since an early age. Thank you to my sister, Tanya, for appreciating my work and always being there when I need someone to listen.

And finally, thank you to my dear cat, Kotia, for inspiring the Curious Cat character.

—Anna

References

Black, T. D. 2022. *ACT for Treating Children: The Essential Guide to Acceptance and Commitment Therapy for Kids.* Oakland, CA: New Harbinger Publications.

Byrne, G., Á. N. Ghráda, T. O'Mahony, and E. Brennan. 2020. "A Systematic Review of the Use of Acceptance and Commitment Therapy in Supporting Parents." *Psychology and Psychotherapy: Theory, Research and Practice* 94(S2): 378–407.

Carter, R. 2020. *How the Brain Works: The Facts Visually Explained.* New York: DK.

Creswell, J. D., W. T. Welch, S. E. Taylor, D. K. Sherman, T. L. Gruenewald, and T. Mann. 2005. "Affirmation of Personal Values Buffers Neuroendocrine and Psychological Stress Responses." *Psychological Science* 16(11): 846–851.

David, A. 2019. *The Secret Life of the Brain: Unlocking the Mysteries of the Mind.* New York: Firefly Books.

De Shazer, S., Y. Dolan, H. Korman, E. McCollum, T. Trepper, and I. K. Berg. 2007. *More Than Miracles: The State of the Art of Solution-Focused Brief Therapy.* Philadelphia: Haworth Press.

Fang, S., and D. Ding. 2020. "A Meta-Analysis of the Efficacy of Acceptance and Commitment Therapy for Children." *Journal of Contextual Behavioral Science* 15: 225–234.

Gilovich, T., K. Savitsky, and V. H. Medvec. 1998. "The Illusion of Transparency: Biased Assessments of Others' Ability to Read One's Emotional States." *Journal of Personality and Social Psychology* 75(2): 332–346.

Gloster, A. T., N. Walder, M. Levin, M. Twohig, and M. Karekla. 2020. "The Empirical Status of Acceptance and Commitment Therapy: A Review of Meta-Analyses." *Journal of Contextual Behavioral Science* 18: 181–192.

Greco, L. A., W. Lambert, and R. A. Baer. 2008. "Psychological Inflexibility in Childhood and Adolescence: Development and Evaluation of the Avoidance and Fusion Questionnaire for Youth." *Psychological Assessment* 20(2): 93–102.

Grosse, G., B. Streubel, C. Gunzenhauser, and H. Saalbach. 2021. "Let's Talk About Emotions: The Development of Children's Emotion Vocabulary from 4 to 11 Years of Age." *Affective Science* 2(2): 150–162.

Hancock, K. M., J. Swain, C. J. Hainsworth, A. L. Dixon, S. Koo, and K. Munro. 2016. "Acceptance and Commitment Therapy Versus Cognitive Behavior Therapy for Children with Anxiety: Outcomes of a Randomized Controlled Trial." *Journal of Clinical Child & Adolescent Psychology* 47(2): 296–311.

Harris, R. 2007. *The Happiness Trap: Stop Struggling, Start Living*. East Gosford, NSW, Australia: Exisle Publishing.

Harris, R. 2019. *ACT Made Simple: An Easy-to-Read Primer on Acceptance and Commitment Therapy*, 2nd ed. Oakland, CA: New Harbinger Publications.

Harris, R. 2022. *The Happiness Trap: How to Stop Struggling and Start Living*, 2nd ed. Boulder, CO: Shambhala Publications.

Hayes, S. C. 2019. *A Liberated Mind: How to Pivot Toward What Matters*. New York: Avery.

Hayes, S. C., and S. Smith. 2005. *Get Out of Your Mind and Into Your Life*. Oakland, CA: New Harbinger Publications.

Hayes, S. C., K. D. Strosahl, and K. G. Wilson. 1999. *Acceptance and Commitment Therapy: An Experiential Approach to Behavior Change*, 1st ed. New York: Guilford Press.

Hayes, S. C., K. D. Strosahl, and K. G. Wilson. 2016. *Acceptance and Commitment Therapy: The Process and Practice of Mindful Change*, 2nd ed. New York: Guilford Press.

Huebner, D. 2006. *What to Do When You Worry Too Much: A Kid's Guide to Overcoming Anxiety*. Washington, DC: American Psychological Association.

Konnikova, M. 2013. *Mastermind: How to Think Like Sherlock Holmes*. New York: Penguin Books.

Latta, S. 2013. *Scared Stiff: Everything You Need to Know About 50 Famous Phobias.* San Francisco: Zest Books.

Locke, E. A., and G. P Latham. 2002. "Building a Practically Useful Theory of Goal Setting and Task Motivation: A 35-Year Odyssey." *American Psychologist* 57(9): 705–717.

Neff, K., and C. Gremer. 2018. *The Mindful Self-Compassion Workbook: A Proven Way to Accept Yourself, Build Inner Strength, and Thrive.* New York: Guilford Press.

Neff, K. D., K. L. Kirkpatrick, and S. S. Rude. 2007. "Self-Compassion and Adaptive Psychological Functioning." *Journal of Research in Personality* 41(1): 139–154.

Palestrini, C., G. Minozzi, S. M. Mazzola, A. Lopez, and S. Cannas. 2022. "Do Intense Weather Events Influence Dogs' and Cats' Behavior? Analysis of Owner-Reported Data in Italy." *Frontiers in Veterinary Science* 9.

Sakakibara, M., J. Hayano, L. O. Oikawa, M. Katsamanis, P. Lehrer, and L. A. Lipsitz. 2013. "Effect of Slowed Respiration on Cardiac Parasympathetic Response to Threat." *Psychosomatic Medicine* 75(3): 3–4.

Siegel, D. J. *Brainstorm: The Power and Purpose of the Teenage Brain.* New York: TarcherPerigee.

Stoddard, J. A., and N. Afari. 2014. *The Big Book of ACT Metaphors: A Practitioner's Guide to Experiential Exercises and Metaphors in Acceptance and Commitment Therapy.* Oakland, CA: New Harbinger Publications.

Sweeney, M. S. 2009. *Brain: The Complete Mind: How It Develops, How It Works, and How to Keep It Sharp.* Washington, DC: National Geographic.

Swift, J. 2014. Путешествия Гулливера *[Gulliver's Travels].* St. Petersburg, Russia: Petroglyph.

Torey, Z. 2014. *Conscious Mind.* Cambridge, MA: MIT Press.

Watts, C., and N. Savona. 2018. *Good Mood Food: Unlock the Power of Diet to Think and Feel Well.* London: Nourish.

About the Author

ANNA SCETININA, MACP, RP, is a registered psychotherapist who lives in Toronto, ON, Canada. Scetinina is a member of the College of Registered Psychotherapists of Ontario (CRPO), and the Ontario Society of Registered Psychotherapists (OSRP). She works at a private practice, providing services to children, adolescents, and adults suffering from stress, perfectionism, low self-esteem, anxiety disorders, obsessive-compulsive disorder (OCD), depression, and more. Scetinina has particular interest and experience in working with children and teens, helping them gradually face social and academic challenges, and develop self-regulatory skills and a flexible mindset through the use of acceptance and commitment therapy (ACT). She is also an award-winning professional artist and graphic designer, incorporating the use of art into her therapeutic approach.

About the Forward Writer

RUSS HARRIS is an internationally acclaimed ACT trainer, and author of the best-selling ACT-based self-help book, *The Happiness Trap*, which has sold more than one million copies and has been published in thirty languages. He is widely renowned for his ability to teach ACT in a way that is simple, clear, and fun—yet extremely practical.

MORE BOOKS from
NEW HARBINGER PUBLICATIONS

**RAISING GOOD
HUMANS EVERY DAY**

50 Simple Ways to Press Pause,
Stay Present, and
Connect with Your Kids

978-1648481420 / US $18.95

**HELPING YOUR
ANXIOUS CHILD,
THIRD EDITION**

A Step-by-Step Guide for Parents

978-1684039913 / US $20.95

**COOPERATIVE
CO-PARENTING FOR
SECURE KIDS**

The Attachment Theory Guide
to Raising Kids in Two Homes

978-1648481840 / US $18.95

**THE ACT WORKBOOK
FOR KIDS**

Fun Activities to Help You Deal with
Worry, Sadness, and Anger Using
Acceptance and Commitment Therapy

978-1648481819 / US $18.95

Instant Help Books
An Imprint of New Harbinger Publications

**THE ANXIETY BUSTING
WORKBOOK FOR KIDS**

Fun CBT Activities to Squash
Your Fears and Worries

978-1648483257 / US $21.95

Instant Help Books
An Imprint of New Harbinger Publications

**THE ANGER
WORKBOOK FOR KIDS**

Fun DBT Activities to Help You
Deal with Big Feelings and
Get Along with Others

978-1684037278 / US $21.95

Instant Help Books
An Imprint of New Harbinger Publications

newharbingerpublications
1-800-748-6273 / newharbinger.com

(VISA, MC, AMEX / prices subject to change without notice)

Follow Us

Don't miss out on new books from New Harbinger.
Subscribe to our email list at **newharbinger.com/subscribe**